I0487777

HOW TO EARN UP TO
$100,000 A YEAR OR
MORE FROM HOME BY MAIL

How To Earn up to $100,000 a Year or More From Home by Mail

The Complete Guide to Starting Your Own Home-Based Mail Order Business

By: Terry Thomas

Writers Club Press

San Jose New York Lincoln Shanghai

How To Earn up to $100,000 a Year or More From Home by Mail
The Complete Guide to Starting Your Own Home-Based Mail Order Business

All Rights Reserved © 2002 by Terry Thomas

No part of this book may be reproduced or transmitted in any form or by any means, graphic, electronic, or mechanical, including photocopying, recording, taping, or by any information storage retrieval system, without the permission in writing from the publisher.

Writers Club Press
an imprint of iUniverse, Inc.

For information address:
iUniverse, Inc.
5220 S. 16th St., Suite 200
Lincoln, NE 68512
www.iuniverse.com

This book is sold as information only. Any statements of income are by no means promises or estimates. They are used for illustrative purposes only. No income guarantees are expressed or implied. Individual results will vary. The author and publisher assume no responsibility or liability resulting from the use of anything presented within this book. You are encouraged to do your own investigation before investing in any business or moneymaking opportunity.

ISBN: 0-595-22055-X

Printed in the United States of America

This book is dedicated to two of the most important people in my life. My Mother Virginia and my beautiful better half, Joy, who's love and support keep me going.

Contents

INTRODUCTION

Hi, thank you for purchasing **How To Earn Up To $100,000 A Year From Home By Mail**. My name is Terry Thomas, the owner of TJT Marketing Associates, a direct marketing company specializing in, among other things, the sale of information and "How To" products via mail order. I look forward to spending some time with you in the pages of this, my newest book. I've been involved in mail order since 1990, really delving into it and forming TJT Marketing Associates in 1995. You may also see our name as TJT Enterprises or TJT Publications. These are all names we have used in the past, although now we try to keep everything under TJT Marketing Associates. We also are associated with the name of my highly regarded monthly newsletter, *Mail Order Marketing News*.

The purpose of this particular book, **How To Earn Up To $100,000 A Year From Home By Mail** is to give you an in-depth look at how to start from nothing and build a mail order business into a full time career. I know it may seem unrealistic to you that one person could make up to $100,000 a year or more from home operating his or her own mail order business. However, let me assure you that it is in fact, very possible. I know because I've done it and so have many other people. Is it easy? Well, heck no. Then again, nothing worth attaining is ever easy. There are folks who complain, "Only 5% of people ever succeed in mail order." Yep, that's probably true, maybe even a little optimistic. However, only 5% of people succeed at ANY career-be it as an athlete, business tycoon, professional or anything else in life. The purpose of this book is to give you the tools and knowledge you need so that YOU can be one of the 5% that succeeds in mail order!

Yes, it is attainable if you dedicate yourself to succeeding and learning and, most importantly, implementing the strategies I am going to present to you in this book.

Actually, this is much more than a simple "book." Along with the other materials you received, it is really a HOME STUDY COURSE on mail order. I've got a lot of "formal" education, including a B.S. and an MBA degree in business. However, that only got me so far. The real reason I succeeded is because of the "street smarts" I picked up and learned along the way, and continue to learn to this day. It is these "street smarts" that make the difference between a successful mail order operator and a failure. Trust me, you CAN be a successful mail order operator. I am going to share my knowledge, both the formal education and the "street smarts" with you in the pages of this book and the related materials that go with it. By the time you are finished **you** are going to be in a position to really make some serious money in mail order, all from your home.

Please take the time to thoroughly read these materials. Much of it may seem a bit overwhelming at first. However, once you finish, you are going to be one of the VERY FEW that know the inside secrets, strategies and knowledge it takes to earn a full time living from home with your own mail order business. I wish you the best of luck in all aspects of your life!

A BRIEF HISTORY OF TJT MARKETING ASSOCIATES

The fact that you have purchased this book tells me that you are look-ing to make some money from home, specifically in mail order. Now, if you are looking to "get-rich-quick" or to suddenly have your mailbox flooded with cash, I am going to burst your bubble right here. It won't happen, doesn't happen and never will happen. Don't believe all the hype in those full-page ads, sales flyers or other promotional materials you see and read everyday. Building your own business, be it mail order or anything else, takes time, patience, dedication, persistence and a sustained effort. A bit of luck here and there never hurts either.

Now, don't get scared and shut the book and quit reading. I tell you this to be up front and honest, the only way I know how to be. If I told you anything different I'd be misleading you. But, and this is a big but, mail order DOES offer you a realistic way to earn a full time income and yes, even become wealthy, in a short period of time when com-pared to other businesses. Mail order has always been, and will con-tinue to be, one of the great entrepreneurial opportunities in existence where the "average Joe" can make a killing–if you know what you are doing. That is the purpose of THIS book.

Why mail order? For many reasons-which I will expound upon in more depth throughout the course of this book. In a nutshell, mail order, also referred to as "direct marketing" or "direct mail" offers the following advantages over many other businesses:

- You can easily enter the mail order industry with few obstacles.

- You can start your own business with very little investment. Yep, even if you are flat broke right now, you can still learn how to create, obtain and sell products via mail order for huge profits.

- You don't need to invest in inventory (unless you want to), employees, pay high rent or purchase a lot of equipment to operate a thriving mail order business.

- No special training, education or fancy degrees are required. Although, as I mentioned previously, a desire to learn and a certain amount of "street smarts" certainly helps.

- You can operate from home, even anonymously if you prefer, and rake in an income equal to or exceeding that of a corporate executive.

- You can start part time, keeping your current job and build your business "on the side" until you are ready to take it full time.

- Mail order is a three hundred billion (yes, that's $300,000,000,000!) dollar a year industry and the potential is limitless. Almost ANYTHING that can be sold via conventional methods can be sold via mail order.

- It's fun!

A Little About Me...

This book is NOT meant to be about me, of course. It is meant to be about YOU and how I can help YOU build your own mail order business. However, I think some background is needed so that you can see how I arrived at this current position in my business life and how you can also do it if you wish.

As I write this part of the book it's about 9:30 on a Tuesday morning. I look outside of my home office on a beautiful mid-winter morning in sunny southern California and the neighborhood is calm. The sun is just starting to make its way into my office, which is really a spare bedroom in our home in an upscale part of town. I spent the better part of last night answering correspondence, filling some orders and doing some writing–until about 11:00 PM–a typical night.

After waking up at 7:00 this morning, I came in the office, turned on the computer, answered some emails, took a couple of phone calls, and watched out my window as my neighbors made their way to work-yuuuck! I remember those days. No more! No more getting dressed up in a monkey suit or fighting the traffic for an hour long commute each way to and from the office. No more dealing with the politics and red tape of the corporate world. Nope, everything I do now is 100% under my control. I shave, take a shower and head back into the office. I answer the phone (it's another order) and make my way to the kitchen for a quick breakfast and a fast read of the morning the paper, then it's back into the office to go to work.

At around noon, I'll take my beloved dog for a walk, clear my mind a bit, and then it's back to work and to see what the day's mail brings. Then, the afternoon is spent filling orders, developing new products and marketing materials, placing ads, scheduling direct mailing campaigns and, literally, counting the day's incoming money! Not a bad life, eh? Especially when you consider that this life allows me to make more money now than I did as a corporate Vice President!

Of course, it's not *all* leisure and fun. My average workday is about 10 hours, with an hour break for my daily work out. There are many 14 or 15 hour workdays, but it's not really "work" at all because it's for me! You see, everybody in this world is selling something. If you go to a job everyday, you are selling your time for money. With mail order, you are selling for yourself and you can control everything you do.

IT WASN'T ALWAYS THIS WAY...

I've ALWAYS been interested in mail order. From the days of the X-Ray Specs in *Boy's Life* to purchasing thousands of dollars in goods via mail. The truth is I actually got "started" in mail order quite by accident about 15 years ago. I remember receiving some sort of advertisement in the mail telling me how this guy's "secret" was going to make me rich. So, I ordered his book. It was by a former truck driver who got rich in mail order selling books and other information. Sounded good, but I had a decent job so it didn't interest me at all. Then, the company I was working for, an import/export management company, started having financial troubles. So, myself and three other executives pooled our money, made arrangements with the bank and, through some help from our customers and vendors, broke off and started our own company. Suddenly, there I was, 28 years old with a business of my own!

The import/export company did well for a couple years, but it was up and down. Because all four of us partners lived all over the place, the office was located some 62 miles from my home, which meant an hour and a half commute each way—what a pain! Anyway, two of our partners dropped out and we bought their interests, and it was just myself and one other partner.

During this time, at a low point in our business, I received an offer in the mail for some "guaranteed money maker"—unbeknownst to me, it was a chain letter program. I remember thinking that "even if I only get 5% of what they claim, I'll still make a fortune!" Big mistake, but it was the start of my mail order education. I joined the program and redid the marketing materials. Man, I was going to make a killing, I just knew it. I purchased a list of names on labels, and my then girl-friend and I spent an entire weekend folding, inserting, stuffing, addressing and stamping 5,000 envelopes. I remember the excitement as I hauled them to the post office. Yep I was going to be rich!

About a week later I received a couple of $10 checks and money orders in the mail. Wow! I thought, this is going to work! One day I got about ten orders—in a single day. Yep, I was on my way boy! Then, nothing, Zippo, dream over. When all was said and done, I'd received about $200 for my efforts—at a cost of over $2,000! But, I was hooked!

Those few checks I received told me that there were, in fact people who would send money for something from someone they didn't even know. I knew that mailing some stupid chain letter or gifting program was not the way to go. It didn't take a genius to figure out the only ones who made money were the promoters of the programs, whether they were legal or not and the mailing list companies selling lists to which these programs were mailed (a revelation that would lead to making me a lot of money at a later date). I went back and dusted off that old mail order book from that former truck driver and started to REALLY study it. Slowly but surely my mail order knowledge increased and I started to form a plan for a new business. But, my other business was so busy I just didn't have the time to start another one, at least not yet.

A couple of years went by and, in an effort to boost the sales of my import/export company, I started selling some products we were importing-via mail order. Nothing major, but it did make us some money. More importantly, I started to put my marketing and advertising education and experience to work in creating ads and sales copy for the products we were selling. We were enjoying some success with the mail order business, but my partner didn't want to be involved with such "piddly stuff" as he called it. So, I was forced to curtail the mail order efforts within our company, but I kept in on the back burner for my own business at some point. So, everything I did with mail order from then on was from my own pocket. Not wanting to give Uncle Sam anymore than necessary I decided to form my own company to pursue the mail order business. So, in 1995 I formed TJT Enterprises, and worked it part time at night and on weekends, from my home selling a few products and "how to" information books and manuals.

Then, I started answering some ads in the business opportunity publications and suddenly started receiving all kinds of offers and publications in the mail. I realized that there was a whole world out there I never knew existed. Publications with hundreds of little display ads and classifieds, touting all kinds of information products. I ordered them left and right, only to find most were complete garbage. However, I also received some very good information about selling information via mail order, and I absorbed it like a sponge.

Over those two or three years, I spent thousands of dollars looking for the "perfect" moneymaker. Mail order programs, liquidating offers, MLM offers, on and on–you name it, I bought it. Eventually, I received an offer from Allen Publishing Company, in Reseda, California. They had a great sales letter advertising for distributors to sell their line of books. Most of the books related to making money or starting a small business and it looked like something I would like to try. I loved the idea that I could just mail out flyers and have orders come to me without having to worry about stocking inventory or shipping anything. When I received orders, I would take my cut and forward the rest to Allen Publishing, who would drop ship the books to my customers. I spent a lot of money in mailings and advertising and received a few orders, but not enough to write home about.

I continued to fiddle around and the one day, from a direct mail piece I received, I ordered a "Mail Order Wealth Building Project" from a company called DAX. Come to find out the owner, Dean F.V. DuVall, Sr. had been at this mail order information business for nearly 35 years! Hey, I thought, now there is someone I could learn from! The "kit" or "project" as it was called, was a program selling DAX's informational products via mail order. You were given the camera-ready masters of his sales flyers, which you copied and distributed. The materials had several of the DAX products advertised on them, along with the DAX address and ordering information, i.e., all the orders went directly to DAX. You simply placed a code you were given (a personal PIN) on the sales materials and when people ordered DAX filled the order and cut you a commission. WOW! I thought, here was a way to offer more products without having to hassle with taking or processing orders. Everything could be done 100% anonymously.

I purchased everything I could from DAX, and studied it thoroughly. I still have the dog-eared books I bought from DAX and refer to them often. But, what really intrigued me was the way they "recruited" other dealers, which they referred to as "Dax-Doers," to market the products for them. For the dealer's efforts, DAX paid a generous commission of 70%. I thought this made more sense than Allen Publishing's deal, so I started promoting them both.

Then one day it hit me like a ton of bricks! I was playing left field for my weekend softball team, when all of a sudden this thought came to me! The KEY to making money was controlling a product of my OWN and having other people help market it for me for a piece of the action! In other words, I needed to be like Allen Publishing Company and DAX! That day I was certainly not "out in left field" because that revelation changed my life forever.

After a few months of study, I decided that the people writing a lot of the articles and publishing the smaller publications really did not know what they were talking about. I was no mail order expert at that point, but I was getting there. Plus, I did have a lot of marketing and advertising experience and figured I could do better than many of the other publications. So, I decided to put together my own little mail order publication offering a combination of editorial content and advertising. So, *Mail Order Marketing News* was born. That first issue, in July 1995 was only two pages. A couple articles on the front, and some ads (all my own, selling the Allen Publishing Books) on the back. I advertised for "co-publishers" or dealers and little by little, orders started coming in. Soon, MOMN, as it came to be called, was 8 full pages, containing $1/2$ ads and $1/2$ articles. I wasn't getting rich with it, but I was getting a name in the mail order industry. I started adding services and products, like typesetting, advertising, copywriting, printing and mailing lists. All of for which I was simply a broker, not a prime source (the one actually producing the product). I eventually put together a complete dealership package for the newsletter and started receiving a lot of orders. I quickly realized that the orders were coming for the dealership and moneymaking opportunity and NOT for the newsletter itself. This is not what I necessarily wanted, but it's what was selling. I eventually decided to cut out all the ads and to this day it remains the ONLY mail order type newsletter of its kind.

So, I began to develop my own products, which I could sell myself and also offer to other people to sell as well. I also continued to offer other people's products on the "back end." Before long I had a nice little offering of products and services and I put together a catalog of all my products and started selling that as well.

About this time, I was going crazy running two businesses and commuting nearly 3 hours everyday. My import business was doing OK, but my partner and I did not see eye to eye on many things. Coincidentally, at that time one of the companies for which we were performing some import services under contract offered my partner a job, since he was the one handling that particular account. He took it; I bought him out and now had sole ownership of both the corporation and my mail order business. For several legal and accounting reasons, I decided to keep them separate.

A few months after buying out my partner, my Dad became ill with cancer and, since my Mom and Dad lived less than a mile from me, I wanted to be around more during the day to help him and my Mom out. Once again, a twist of bad luck turned into my good fortune. In my import business, I had a decent sized warehouse which we used for distribution of our customer's products–just one of the things we did as a company. Anyway, the company for whom we were distributing these products for was sold to another company who already had a warehouse in southern California, so they didn't need us anymore. That was my opening, and I jumped on it. I helped my employees find jobs with an associated company, then closed the warehouse and moved the entire operation into my home. I got to spend a lot of time with Dad in his final days (even though I'd always spent a lot of time with him, it was special) before he passed away in August 1996. Plus, I was now free to really explore and build my mail order business.

In just five years I went from doing just a few thousand dollars a year in mail order to doing well over $150,000 a year in sales. All from my home, all without the need for full time employees. While I continue to run and operate both my import and mail order businesses, it is now my mail order business that receives most of my time and attention. It's exciting, fun and I continue to be amazed at the unlimited profit potential from my mail order business.

One final thing I want to say before we move on. Long ago, when I was being pummeled with so much B.S. from all the so-called "experts" out there I decided that I really wanted to help people. As Zig Ziglar once said: "You can get whatever you want in life if you'll just show others how to get what they want." Or, as one of my mentor's Dean DuVall of DAX said way back in 1969: "To reach the top of the success ladder, one must grasp the next rung firmly with one hand, whilst extending the other to the fellow below." Quite a powerful philosophy and one in which I truly believe. My point is this; I always told myself that if I ever achieved any level of success, in anything, I would share that success with others. I believe everybody should have the same opportunity to get rich and be happy. That is my real motivation for writing this book and all the others I have written, in addition to continuing to publish my monthly newsletter, *Mail Order Marketing News*. Do I know all there is to know? Heck no, but I know more than most. And what I DO know has afforded me the opportunity to make a very good living from the comfort of my home. You too can achieve this dream and I want to help show you how! Remember, all I can do is show you—the rest is up to you.

GETTING STARTED

Just what is "mail order" anyway? Mail order, or direct marketing as it is usually referred to, is nothing more than a means of selling goods and services. It doesn't matter if the person orders from a catalog sent directly to him, one he picks up from a store, and advertisement he sees in a magazine or other publication or from a printed or telephone solicitation he receives in the mail. If a customer orders something, anything, and it is delivered via "mail" or another type of delivery service, it is classified as mail order. While direct marketing may be the more correct term, encompassing all kinds of scenarios, it's still just good old mail order in one form or another. And, as stated before, the mail order market is HUGE. Think of your own purchases over the years. How many were from a catalog, advertisement or television commercial? Probably quite a few I would guess. So, now you know that mail order is, in fact, big business. The question that is probably burning in your own mind is. "How in the world can I enter this industry and make some money at it?" Ah, the big $100,000 question. Well, let's see if we can help you answer that question…

First of all you need to figure out just how involved you wish to be, for it will determine where you go from here. Do you want to act solely as an independent sales agent, selling other people's products? Or, do you want to form your own company with the ability to sell your own products, other's products or any combination thereof? Well, if you just want to act as an independent agent you will need to do nothing more than contact those types of companies and ask for a "distributor" or "dealer" kit. They will usually send you a bunch of master copies of their own sales materials for the products they market. These are called "camera ready" advertising materials. All this means is that they are ready to be shot by a "camera" in order to make a printing plate for duplication. More on that later. Right now, the point is that you are now entitled to solicit orders on that company's behalf, for which you are paid a commission.

If you do this, or any other business opportunity, understand that there is only so much a company can do for you. They can only give you the tools. It is up to you to turn those tools into a profitable venture. My mail order friends and I often lament about how most opportunity seekers really are not looking for a business opportunity at all. They still have the "job" mentality that they are going to trade their time for money. Doesn't work that way in your own business. You have to take control to earn your own living. It's kind of like fishing. If you want to be a fisherman you need to have someone teach you, then go out and do it. But, don't expect someone to give you the instructions on how to fish and then, on top of it all, provide you with the boat, the rod and reel, all the equipment and then throw the fish into your boat besides. No my friend, actually going out and catching the fish is up to you. A legitimate business opportunity works the same way. All anyone can give you is information and knowledge, how you use it is up to you. But, this is what makes starting your own mail order business so exciting–because it is really "up to you" to succeed!

Be aware that many companies will charge for a distributor kit. Nothing wrong with that, as long as the only reason they are charging is NOT to recruit more investors and have you do the same. In other words if the only way you make money is by selling the "kit" to others forget it. It's not only an illegal chain program, it will never make you a dime.

You can pick up some nice extra cash acting as strictly an agent or dealer for other people's products. However, unless your selling something with a high profit margin and commission structure (for example, mailing lists) you are probably not going to make enough to really earn a full time living. This is where forming your OWN company makes sense. Since this book is about how to earn up to $100,000 or more a year from home by mail, we will assume that you wish to start your own company. So, what do you do now?

First of all, you need to decide which type of entity you wish to be, i.e. a corporation, partnership, sole proprietorship, S corporation or Limited Liability corporation (LLC). If you don't understand the difference between these, I suggest you check with an accountant or attorney. Most likely you are going to start a sole proprietorship or partnership. These are the easiest and the ones most new, home-based entrepreneurs choose. You can always incorporate at a later date if you wish. The main reason for incorporating is to form a new entity with it's own identity–separate from yours. This gives you some legal protection against any liabilities you may incur–such as lawsuits. However, this does not mean you can form a corporation, run up all kinds of bills and have no liability for them. Small corporations are almost always forced to sign personal guarantees from the officers against any liabilities incurred.

Anyway, all of that is beyond the scope of this book. No matter which form of business you choose, you first need to come up with a name. Take your time coming up with a name. It could be something as simple as Joe Smith Publications, or anything you choose. Try not to sound too cute or hokey. You want people to view you as a serious business. Now, if you choose ANY name other than your own given name you MUST file a fictitious business statement. This is a public filing telling people that you are conducting business under an assumed, or "fictitious" name. Contact your city hall or county clerk for information on this filing. Or, you can contact your local newspaper and ask them for information about filing a Fictitious Name Business Statement. For a flat fee, they will handle everything for you.

Next, check with your local authorities at city hall or the county clerk's office about any other licenses you may need, such as a business license. Every local and municipality is different and some might even have restrictions about conducting a business from your home, so be sure and check it out first.

Now, once you have your Fictitious Business Statement filed and any licenses you need, go to your bank and open up a business checking account. DO NOT use you personal account for business purposes. You want to take advantage of all the tax savings you can and you want to be sure you keep your personal and business activities separate—and so does the IRS! Never mix up your business expenses with your personal expenses or visa versa. Keep them totally separate. Now, order some business size checks. Don't use the small, personal size checks. You want to appear professional and the commercial type business size checks always look more credible.

Next, get yourself some business stationery—letterhead, envelopes, business cards, etc. You can order these very cheaply an office supply store or, if you have a computer and quality printer, you can even get by in the beginning printing letterhead and business cards from your computer. Do NOT use a rubber stamp for your envelopes, and by all means don't hand write your return address. It costs little more to have your name and address printed on your envelopes. If you have online access, you can visit **www.iprint.com**. You can design, edit and order ALL your business correspondence needs—including checks, letterhead, envelopes, business cards, forms and anything else you can think of. The prices are competitive and the quality of work is excellent.

Finally you need to choose an address. You can use your home address as your business address. However, it is prudent to either rent a PO Box from your local Post Office or from an independent service, such as Mail Boxes, etc. With the latter you can still have the appearance of a "street" address and also can use them to accept UPS and similar shipments. There are many people who say a PO Box will hurt your business and that people will think you are "hiding" behind a PO Box. This is not necessarily as true today as it was a few years back. The point is, anybody can find out the owner and street address of a business PO Box by simply writing the Post Office and requesting that information. A PO Box offers many benefits, including faster delivery of your mail, ability to access you box at any time and it maintains some sort of security. You would not necessarily want everyone in your hometown dropping by your home for business purposes. This is one of the reasons you are in "mail order" and not some other business. Plus, when you start writing classified ads, which charge by the word, it's cheaper to use a Box number because it saves at least a word or two.

SETTING UP YOUR HOME-BASED MAIL ORDER OFFICE

Those of us that work out of our homes realize that it can be a double-edged sword. Yes, we enjoy the freedom of a home-office, no commuting, and a totally flexible schedule. But, this also means that we must budget our time, work efficiently, and commit ourselves to working smart.

First of all, "home-business" does not necessarily mean "small" business in terms of revenue. There are many home-businesses that are multi-million dollar corporations. I know, because I run one from my home. IMC, Inc. is an import/export company, which I now own 100% and run from my home. It grosses over one million dollars in sales per year! Sure, I have a separate warehouse, but the business is RUN from my home!

Operating two companies from home is not always easy, but the benefits easily outweigh the negative aspects. I have learned to work effectively from home, and want to share some things that I feel will enable you to get the most out of your home-based business or office.

First of all, you must create a totally separate room or area to be used exclusively for business. If you do not have a basement, garage, or spare room, partition an area in one of the other rooms. Designate this as your "office", and treat it as such. Do not use it for anything but work! And, even more importantly, do not go in there unless you are going to "work". Why? Because if you treat the office area as a separate entity, you will be more productive. Make sure that your family members know it is an "office" and is off limits to them! The more separate you can make your office area, the better off you will be, and the more professional a business you can run.

There are some things that I feel are absolutely necessary to outfit a home office. First of all is space. As I mentioned, do the best you can with what is available. A spare room, garage, attic, or basement is best. But, if this is not feasible, a partitioned area of a room will do.

Depending on the level and sophistication of your mail order business, you may wish to have a separate phone line installed. This will make it easier for customers to reach you, and will project a more professional image. A fax machine is certainly a must for some businesses. For example, my import/export company could not function without one. Although preferable, you not need a separate phone line for your fax. You can use a telephone-sharing device, which automatically routes calls to a phone, fax, or modem. These are readily available, and eliminate the need to have a dedicated fax line. Of course, if you receive a high volume of phone calls or faxes, you will need a couple of phone lines. You might even want to lease a multi-line phone system from the telephone company. All of this will come in time if it is necessary.

Next, a personal computer is a must as your mail order business grows. It is difficult to run any sort of successful business without a computer. Invest in the best one that you can afford. Computer prices are dropping every day, and it is possible to get a very powerful system for under $700. If you cannot afford a new one, look for a used one or lease one. You will also need a printer capable of printing legible correspondence. If you want to create your own brochures, ads, or high quality correspondence you should get a laser printer.

As far as furniture is concerned, make sure you have a desk that is large enough to handle your needs, and a file cabinet or two for your files. Most importantly, get a good, comfortable chair. *Yes, this can be your most important office tool!* Get the best chair you can afford. Many back and neck problems and fatigue are caused by a cheaply made chair.

Finally, if feasible you can purchase an office copier. This is not necessary, as there are numerous copy places in every community. But, to save time and money, if you are going to do a lot of copying you should invest in your own copier. Just one that will handle everyday copying is fine. Any larger jobs can still be done at your local print or copy shop.

Set up a regular working schedule, even if it's only part time for now. Eventually, if you're like me, you'll be working at all hours of the night. Still, just like if you had to go to a regular job, set up some "business hours". If you are going to have hours from 9:00 AM to 5:00 PM, then stick to that schedule! Go into your office from 9 to 5, every day, just as if you were going to a regular place of employment. Take normal breaks, including lunch. But, it is important that you establish a regular habit of being "in the office" on a set schedule every day. Of course there will be times you must leave the office to make sales calls, run errands, or for other reasons. When you are out make sure that there is an answering machine to answer any incoming calls, and that you return the calls as soon as you return.

Make sure your family and friends are aware of your regular "business" hours. Ask them to respect that time, just as if you were at work. They should not expect you to be "free" all the time just because you are at home. Most of all, make sure that you yourself respect those office hours! Of course there will be times when you might want to play golf, take some time to yourself, or just relax. After all, this is one of the benefits of working at home. But, you must realize that time is money, and judge your leisure time accordingly! If you take too much leisure time, you will not be successful-no matter what type of home business you have!

When you get up in the morning, act as if you are going to work! Shower and get dressed as if you are going to a place of employment. Many people actually wear a tie, or business suit to make them feel more professional. You do not have to go to this extreme, but you should not work in your underwear either, although you certainly could with your mail order business. If you dress like you are going to work, you will feel more like working! Also, if you ever have customers or vendors visit you at your "office" you want to appear as professional as possible.

Outfit your office as best you can within your budget. Treat it as a business, and work regular hours. Your business or office may be at home, but it is still an "office"! Treat it like a professionally run place of business!

RECORD KEEPING

It's beyond the scope of this book to fully educate you on record keeping and accounting procedures. If you are not familiar with accounting, you may want to consult an outside accountant or hire a bookkeeper to set up your accounting and keep track of your records. However, I do want to give you some basics.

First of all, you need to get yourself a ledger book (or you can even use a notebook to start) to keep track of all your cash receipts and cash outlays. Be sure to clearly mark what each transaction related to. For example, your book might look like this:

Date	Transaction	Receipt	Payment	Reference
01/31/01	J. Jones/Order	25.00		CK# 107
01/31/01	Sam's Printing Inv 1035		155.00	CK# 100

You should also keep a very clean and accurate checkbook. The most important thing is to be able to track the money you take in and the money you pay out and the details of the receipt or payment. Make it a habit from the very beginning to keep accurate records. It will save you a lot of time and headaches in the long run. You may even want to computerize your accounting at some point. There are several software programs that can help you do this. QuickBooks and PeachTree Accounting are two of the more popular programs.

You should also include an invoice with every order shipped. This can be done on the computer (several programs available to do this, including the aforementioned accounting software programs) or, at the very least, get a book of general sales order or invoice forms from your local office supply store and use those. Keep one copy for your records and include the other one with the order you ship to your customer. You should also, if possible, make a copy of the order form from the customer for your records. Attach it to your copy of the invoice. Create a file for all invoices, checks, etc. Create separate files for those vendors and customers with whom you do a lot of business.

SHIPPING ORDERS

Shipping orders is an important part of your customer service and how the order is shipped reflects upon you and your company. First of all, try to ship all orders as soon as possible–within 24 hours is best. If you are sending the order to a prime source to have it drop shipped, do it quickly and insist that the prime source ships quickly as well. With drop shipping, you should send the customer an acknowledgement of the order informing him or her that the order will be shipped directly from the manufacturer.

By law you must ship orders within 30 days. If you are delaying an order more than 30 days you must notify the customer, in writing that the order will not ship within 30 days and give them an estimated shipping date. You must also give them the option to cancel the order.

The method of shipping you use is up to you. For information products and smaller products you can probably get by shipping them all by mail. If the order has a high dollar value, you may want to insure the shipment and also obtain a proof of delivery. For heavier items and larger shipments you can ship via UPS. UPS will pick up your shipments on an "as needed" basis, or you can set up an account and regular pick-up service. Contact UPS at 1-800-PICKUPS for more information, or visit their Web Site at **www.ups.com**.

Be sure to pack your orders securely so that they arrive in good shape. Use a pre-printed shipping label and be sure your return address is clearly indicated. Your package should arrive looking like it was packed with care–not sloppy.

Okay, now that you have your business structure in place, chosen your company name, obtained any applicable licenses, filed your Fictitious Business Statement and opened your bank account–you're in business! Now, place a few ads and wait by the phone for the orders to come pouring in. Just joking, I wish it were that simple. Unfortunately, many people do think it's that simple and that's why they fail to ever get the business going. No, you've got to make it happen, but now the real fun begins! Before I get into the nitty gritty I want to implore upon you the importance of taking your business seriously and working hard to make your dreams come true. It can happen, but only if you MAKE it happen. I want to share a true story with you…

A TRUE STORY OF TWO MAIL ORDER ENTREPRENEURS

A few years back, about 1995 or 1996 I suppose, I had two new mail order entrepreneurs contact me at about the same time. I was just starting to gain some notoriety and credibility from my newsletter, *Mail Order marketing News* and through articles I wrote which were starting to show up in the major (and not so major) business opportunity publications. Anyway, one way or another these two gentlemen got a hold of my name and phone number and called me. It was the beginning of two long business relationships for me–one good, the other a disaster. In order to protect the identities of these two folks, I'll refer to them as Larry Winner and Barry loser–LW and BL for short. Both had about the same experience in mail order when they first called me. Neither had anything more than a high school education and no formal business training or education.

Anyway, Larry Winner called me first. I distinctly remember the call because we seemed to hit it off right away. LW had a lot of questions for me, based on an article of mine he had just read. He wanted to know about placing ads, what he should ask for in the ad (a self addressed stamped envelope, stamps, cash) what he should write in the ad and all kinds of other intelligent questions. I answered him with my opinions, some of which he may have agreed with, some he may not have agreed with. But he took it all in and I could tell he was making notes. He never disagreed openly, only asking me intelligent questions. We had a pleasant conversation that day and we talked often in subsequent months.

Over the years, LW became one of my very good friends. The thing about LW is he never stopped doing things and testing. He always asked questions and thought about the replies, without argument. He would then use his own judgment as to what he would use and what he would discard. LW took his business seriously and he had a plan. He worked hard and consistently, never resting on his successes. He continued to work his normal jobs while he built his mail order business, pouring all the profits back into his business and not depending on his mail order income for survival. We started to share many things in business and did many things together as he became more and more experienced. It was always a pleasure to speak with LW and share in his success as his business grew.

Barry Loser first called me just a few weeks after LW. He was openly disagreeing with something I had written in one of my articles. No problem, disagreements are welcome. But he, in this case, was speaking from total inexperience and really didn't know what he was talking about. I could tell he had zero experience with mail order or business. Yet, each time I would answer his questions he would argue that I was wrong and his answer was right. OK, then why ask the question? He said he wanted to learn, but he really didn't want to hear any advice he disagreed with. BL really rubbed me the wrong way, but I felt sorry for him and tried to help him the best I could. Over the years BL had a little success, but then would be stubborn and try to do things his way without heeding advice from others. His business never took off. He depended on his business for survival and refused, for one reason or another, to get a job to help support him and his family while his business grew. The little profits he made he had to use to survive, so little went back into the business. BL was a critical person who belittled other's success and thought he knew it all. The more I tried to help and give things to BL it seemed the more he wanted. He seemed destined to remain where he was in business, with little chance for growth.

So, where are they now? Well, the last I heard BL was in severe financial trouble and was no longer doing much in mail order. He was still searching for that "magic lantern" I suppose. LW, on the other hand, is now one of the most successful sellers of money making and business opportunity information. He long ago quit his jobs and survives entirely on his mail order business income, which is now well over $20,000 per month. He continues to be one of my closest friends and allies in this business.

So, what's the moral here? Simple. Be open to new challenges and learn from those that have gone ahead of you. Try to absorb as much knowledge as you can. You don't always have to agree with the opinions of those you interact with, but instead of being critical and thinking you know it all, dedicate yourself to improving a little everyday. Don't expect your mail order business to support you right away. Keep your current job and work your mail order business part time if necessary, reinvesting all your profits back into your business in order to give it a chance to grow. If something's not working, change direction a little bit and be open to new suggestions. Respect people you interact with in the business and give back whenever possible. Form positive relationships with those people whom can help you build your business. Best of all, be like Larry Winner above and less like Barry Loser. Larry Winner is proof positive what can happen in mail order when you have a clear vision, a willingness to learn and a desire to work hard AND smart in order to get what you want.

THE SECRET OF LEVERAGING YOURSELF

In order to truly achieve financial success in any business, especially mail order, you must learn to leverage yourself. What exactly do I mean by leverage? I mean you must have the ability to duplicate your product or service many times over. You need to find a way to system-ize your business so that it could be replicated 5,000 times, and the 5,000th unit would run as smoothly as the first. In other words, you need to clone yourself, your product, or your service!

Think about it. No matter what business you are in or no matter how hard you work, you are limited by one variable that you cannot do anything about-time. Think of an attorney, charging one hundred dol-lars an hour. Let's say he works very hard, and bills eight hours a day, five days a week. This works out to $4,000 per week, or $208,000 per year. Not a bad living by any means. But, he does not have any time to do anything else, and no matter how much harder he works he will always be limited by the amount of time he has. Now, take that same attorney, and put him in charge of a law firm with ten partners. He teaches his partners his strategies for landing new clients and has them duplicate his system. Say they each bill only 5 hours a day and share the revenue 50/50 with the head of the firm. Now the firm is billing a total of $25,000 per week, or $1,300,000 per year. The head attorney gets $650,000 per year, and he does not have to bill one hour himself! This is an example of how leverage works! This is the same principal that any successful business is based upon-the idea of leveraging a product or a system of doing business.

It works in mail order too! Whatever product you have, or whatever service you are offering, chances are you can utilize the principal of leverage to further your success. How? Think about what you are selling. Are you trying to do it on your own? Let's say you have a great how to book that is a great seller at $20. You are selling 1,000 books a month for a gross revenue of $20,000. Not bad, but you are limited by what you can do on your own. Now, let's say that you allow the book to be sold by dealers and you give them 50% of the sales revenue. You duplicate your sales efforts, and all of your sales materials. If you sign up 10 dealers, and they sell only 500 books a month each, you are grossing $50,000 per month! And, you can gross this while playing golf, vacationing, or sitting on your couch. Better yet, you can utilize the time to develop new marketing programs. Your dealers are happy because they are making money and have access to a saleable product. And you are happy because you have increased your sales, and your profits, while spending LESS time!

Consider another example. If you are a lecturer and average $1,000 per day for a seminar, you are making $5,000 per week. But, you can only give so many seminars because you are only one person. What if you take that seminar and make it into a video or book and sell it for $20? You are now duplicating your efforts, and can reach a multitude of new customers, allowing you to reap many times more profits!

Almost every millionaire in this country realizes the importance of leverage. They know that one person is limited by time constraints and cannot possibly reach the number of customers that can be reached through a well-devised leverage situation.

Of course it takes time to be in a position to really use leverage to your advantage. The point is, you should recognize what it is, and know how to utilize it when you are ready. Most successful mail order operators have used this principal for years to increase their sales. Some of the great ones come to mind, the really heavy hitters like Melvin Powers, Dean F.V. DuVall, and others. They have used leverage for years by selling what they know to other people, who then solicit new business for them. DuVall is a classic case of leverage used to the greatest degree. Dean, head of DAX Financial Publications, long ago realized the potential of using leverage. He packaged his seminars, his moneymaking systems, and various other great discoveries into books and other publications, which he sells through a network of dealers. He pays his dealers up to 70% commissions, yet he makes a fortune because he has numerous dealers selling his products. He has been at it for 40 years now and is still a top name in the industry. His numerous successes are well documented in his many books and publications.

Remember, the only way to succeed in mail order is to sell more products! Sure you can cut your costs, become more efficient, or increase your profit margins. But, the bottom line is that mail order is and always has been a numbers game. In order to truly succeed you have to reach a greater number of people, and sell a greater number of your product or service! You can spend a fortune, and work 24 hours a day trying to peddle your products or services, but time and even money will always limit you. By utilizing the principal of leverage, you can multiply yourself many times over! You can multiply either your product or service, or you can multiply a marketing system. Either way, the point is that you can utilize the time, talents, and sales efforts of many others to increase your bottom line.

People are always looking for a way to make money. If you have a viable product, service or marketing system that you can duplicate, they will be more than happy to help you.

Once you have a product or service that is selling, and you have utilized the principal of leverage to the maximum degree, you will truly have it made. For then you will have what I consider the greatest reward of success-FREE TIME! This is what it is all about! Time to spend with friends and family, time to spend as you want. For any time that is spent doing what you want to do is never wasted time.

WHAT PRODUCTS TO SELL

This is one of the most confusing things to people starting out, what products should you sell? The answer is rarely clear-cut, but you'll save yourself a lot of headaches and be much more enthusiastic about your business if you sell products in which YOU have an interest. For example, if you like sports you may start with sports related products. The more knowledge and experience you have with a particular product category, the better your chance of succeeding when trying to sell it via mail order. You are also more apt to stick with something in which you have an affinity with or enjoy.

Now, you can sell actual, tangible products if you so choose. Many people do and they make a lot of money doing it. However, be aware that the product must be something with a lot of profit built in to it, so you can sell it via mail order and cover all your advertising and marketing expenses. Plus, it must be a product that is unique in some way—i.e., not something your customer could just buy at the local discount store. You are not going to be successful competing with your local Wal-Mart

The product I love to sell and one that I advocate is information. People LOVE information and will buy it in droves and, thankfully, spend a lot of money to obtain it. You can easily put together a book or other information product for just a few dollars and sell it for up to $30 or more. This allows you enough of a profit margin to not only make money yourself, but also to form a network of dealers to sell it as well and still earn a substantial commission or profit for their efforts—more on this later.

No matter what products you choose to sell, there are three basic ways for you to obtain those products:

Manufacture Your Own Product–This means you actually develop or manufacture a product–be it informational or other type–and maintain an inventory and ship it all yourself. If you choose to manufacture or create a product on your own, make sure you price the product at a level that covers ALL your expenses.

Purchase Products Wholesale And Resell Them–This is certainly a possibility for you if you are looking to enter mail order without having to create or come up with your own product. You purchase at wholesale price from the manufacturer, inventory the product and then resell it at retail. Be careful when purchasing wholesale to be sure the products you are buying can be readily sold at a price level that allows you to make enough profit. The last thing you want to do is buy a bunch of product and then get "stuck" with it.

Using The "Drop Ship" Method–This is probably the best way to start if you are selling tangible products and have not yet come up with your "own" product to sell. This is also a great way to broaden your product offering without having to purchase inventory or invest more money. Under this method you contact suppliers of the products you wish to sell and obtain permission to sell those products. You are responsible for the marketing and advertising. Many times, the "Prime Source" (the actual supplier of the product) will provide you with marketing materials you can use. You obtain orders, keep your profit and send the wholesale price to the prime source along with one of YOUR shipping labels pre-addressed to your customer. The prime source then "drop ships" (ships it directly to your customer on your behalf) to your customer using YOUR shipping label. We'll discuss drop shipping in more detail a little later on.

Whatever method you choose, or if you choose a combination of all three, remember one secret to mail order: **THE REAL PROFITS**

COME FROM MAKING ADDITIONAL SALES TO EXISTING CUSTOMERS–CALLED "BACK-END" SALES. You are never going to survive selling just one product, unless that product is 100% consumable (gets used up over and over) and has a HUGE profit margin. No, you are going to have to sell more than one product. This is not as difficult as it sounds, as you will learn as you continue reading this book.

So, where do you find products to sell? This is not as hard as it may seem. In fact, finding products is the easy part. Products are everywhere. You can start by visiting the local library and looking through certain directories, such as *The Thomas Register*, which lists the sources of thousands of manufacturers and distributors of various products. You could also contact trade associations and ask them for information about the companies who are members of the organization. You can look in magazines and see what is being offered from different companies, or in catalogs. Write or call the suppliers and ask them if they have a distributor or dealer program or, if you want to purchase the products for resale, ask them for a wholesale price list.

My suggestion, as I said, is to start with information. There are literally hundreds of thousands of manuals, books, tapes, CD's, and other information products available for resale. Or, you can contact a company and ask for permission to reprint or resell what they are offering. This is a common practice in the "opportunity information" industry.

Whatever you sell, stick to the proven product categories such as: self-improvement, health, financial improvement, sex and health, beauty, business opportunities and the like. These are ALL products people use and purchase all the time. There is a huge demand for them and the market is extensive.

DON'T COMPETE AGAINST YOURSELF

If you're going to sell something by direct marketing you need to have some sort of marketing advantage. In other words, you need to differentiate your product in such a way that it makes it logical and appealing for your customer to purchase it via direct mail as opposed to buying it at the local discount store. This can be done in a number of ways, the most common being price. If you can sell a well-known product at a price much lower than conventional retail outlets, you have a marketing advantage. Another common way to achieve an advantage is to sell a product that is unique and cannot be purchased just anywhere, maybe even exclusively from you.

One of the biggest mistakes you can make is to try and sell a product only to find others selling the same product for much less. This kills many smaller mail order dealers because they simply cannot compete against large discount retail operations. If you are buying a product for $15 and the local Wal Mart sells it for $19.95 you'll obviously fail because you cannot make a profit. This happens all the time, especially on some of the popular "fad" items.

I'll give you an example. About a year ago I started seeing this commercial for a singing bass fish that is mounted on a wooden plaque. It is motion activated and when someone walks by it turns its head and starts singing. I think it's a hoot, and a clever gift item. Anyway, it was being sold exclusively via TV ads for $29.99. Before long, I started seeing it in catalogs for $29.99 or even $24.99–a good deal. However, it did not take long before it was being sold on TV for $19.99. Now that $24.99 in the catalog wasn't such a great deal after all. If the catalog had a large inventory they would have no choice but to lower their price, thereby lowering their profit margin. But it did not end there. The other day I was in my local OSH Hardware store and saw this same item for $12.97! Now that catalog company selling the item for $24.99 was WAY out of line and would end up losing a lot of money. They were, in essence, competing against themselves, or at least against their own product.

Now it's no secret that a lot of this is planned marketing by those "As Seen On TV" companies. You see, they find a hot product and hock it on TV, controlling the distribution rights. Once they saturate the market at a higher price from the TV ad, they release the product into the mainstream catalogs and retail outlets. At the same time, they drop the price on the TV ads. Eventually, the TV ads disappear and they sell the product for an even lower price via catalogs and retail outlets. How about those "Tap Lights" that sold for $19.99 each? You can buy a package of six of them now for $9.99. It's the same principal. If you see anything new advertised for direct sale on TV, I suggest you wait about three months or so. You'll then be able to buy it for much less.

This is a smart marketing practice if you are the one controlling the product. However, if you are purchasing the product for resale and suddenly you see it being sold for less than you can buy it for, you are in some trouble.

THE "PERFECT" MAIL ORDER PRODUCT

Competition in direct marketing is fierce, especially with fad items. That is why information is the perfect item to sell via mail order. Your costs are very low to produce, yet the perceived value is quite high. You can sell the items for huge profits and not be stuck with an acquisition cost that may be higher than the current market price in just a short time. Best of all, if it is YOUR information product, you control the price and the distribution. This means you won't end up competing against yourself. Even if you are selling somebody else's product, you can customize your own sales materials so that it is not obvious you are selling the same thing as everybody else.

The only thing you do have to be careful about is if you happen to be lucky enough to get a publishing deal. This is great, unless your book doesn't sell. There's nothing worse than trying to sell your book for $19.95 only to find it in the remainder bin at your local bookstore for $2.95. However, even if something like this were to happen, your exposure is much less when selling information. In other words, it is not like that singing bass that everybody with a TV has seen and knows how much it sells for.

Whenever anyone asks me what he or she should sell via mail order, I steer him or her in the direction of information. It is so much easier to sell than consumer products and you rarely end up competing with yourself. Of course there are exceptions to everything. For example, if you are a catalog like Damark which specializes in selling closeouts or popular items at discount prices you can certainly be successful selling consumer products that are available any number of places because you are selling it at a much lower price. However, you'll notice these catalogs sell these popular products AFTER they have started their market decline. In other words, the manufacturers wait until they sold as many as they could at a higher cost before selling to the discounters.

You run a great risk selling products if you buy a lot of them during the beginning of the product's life cycle. If you get in quick and can buy a minimal amount you can ride the popularity wave of the product. However, don't commit to a large quantity of any product or else you'll end up with products you cannot sell at a profit. This is another reason to stick to selling information.

PROTECT YOUR DEALERS

Once you become the prime source of a product, which is necessary for your success, as you will learn later on, you will most likely use dealers and distributors. It is important that you protect them from low-balling prices. For example, if you sell an item for $20 and you sell it to your dealers for $10, you would not want to run a promotion selling the product direct for $12. This is not fair to your dealers and will certainly not give you a very good reputation.

You need to protect your dealers whether you are selling information or other products. Set dealer prices and retail prices and make sure you stick to them. If a dealer wants to sell for a lower price and reduce his or her profit margin, that is up to them. Sure, you might have dealers competing against one another but that's just business. It's no different than Sears competing with K-Mart on name brand merchandise. However, you should not compete directly with your own dealers by selling your product directly to consumers at a price point much lower than the retail price.

Competition is good and it is healthy for your business. However, it is one thing to compete against another company. It is much harder when you end up competing against your own products. The more you can control your product sourcing and distribution, the better off you will be.

USING DROP SHIPPING TO BUILD PROFITS!

OK, so you decide to enter the mail order business. Or maybe you are already in the business, but want to expand your operation. You may even have a product in mind to sell. But, you get discouraged because you know you cannot afford the cost of inventory, storage, shipping, order processing, employees, and so on. What do you do? Abandon your project? Borrow money for inventory and expenses? Wait for a rich uncle to drop dead and leave you a fortune? Well, you could, but the easiest way is to use DROP SHIPPING!

Drop shipping simply means that a supplier will ship orders to someone other than the person actually making the purchase. This is a viable option for mail order operators that cannot afford, or do not wish to carry inventory. It is also an excellent way to "test" certain products, since you do not have to purchase inventory first. Many companies are willing to offer you dealership giving you the right to sell their products. All types of products are sold this way. The most common, and profitable, are "how to" books, manuals, and tapes, novelty items, and gift products.

Most drop ship agreements are simple. You find the customers, and obtain the orders. When you get an order, you deduct your profit (usually 50%) and send the remaining money, along with a shipping label to the drop shipper. They then send the order directly to your customer, using your mailing label. As far as your customer is concerned, the order came directly from YOU.

Most suppliers will charge you a small "fee" to be an established dealer for their products. They usually supply you with camera-ready circulars or other advertising material. You are responsible for the costs of obtaining the customers, including printing, advertising, postage costs, etc. The main advantage to you is that you do not have to pay for any merchandise until you actually sell it. You can find a list of companies who drop ship by obtaining a copy of *The American Drop Shippers Directory*, available at most libraries.

The most important thing is to be sure that you choose your suppliers very carefully. Investigate the company, and talk to other dealers if possible. Be sure they are legitimate. Most companies may charge you the dealership fee, which is fine because it means you are serious. But, beware of the companies that force you to buy printed sales material, or mailing lists directly from them. These companies are not interested in selling their products. Instead, they make money on the dealership fees and by selling printing and mailing lists!

THE KEY TO SELLING PRODUCTS YOU DON'T PRODUCE

If you're going to be successful selling products by mail order you have to be the prime source—at least that's what all the "experts" would lead you to believe. This is not necessarily true. When most people get into "mail order" they start by selling information, which is a prudent thing to do. Information is easily obtained, inexpensive to produce, in high demand and can be sold for huge profits. However, if you are not the "prime source" of the book, manual, report or tape that you are selling, there is going to be less of a profit margin for you. This means that in order to succeed you are going to either have to charge more, or fine-tune your marketing so that you obtain more sales.

Many so-called "experts" tell you there is no way you can make money selling other's products. They whine that, after all, you are the one doing "all the work", including advertising, marketing, etc. This is true—but only to a certain extent. Believe me, developing a successful product that fills a market need takes a lot of time and development. The prime source also has production expenses, inventory storage and handling, administrative costs, shipping and a myriad of other associated overhead costs. So, the dealer is not doing "all the work". As a dealer or distributor, you are doing your part to obtain customers. This is no different than the local sporting goods store selling Nike shoes. They benefit from Nike's advertising and promotion, of course. However, if they don't market themselves in order to draw customers into the store, they are not going to sell anything.

So, yes you CAN make money selling products that you do not produce. However, the best associations are with prime sources that will help you with your marketing efforts with co-op advertising and other "pull-through" marketing techniques.

THE REAL SECRET DOES NOT INVOLVE THE PRODUCT

I've said it many times–finding a product to sell is not that difficult, once you learn what to look for. There are many products, both information type and tangible consumer products, which fill a particular need. The key to selling anything by mail is NOT to necessarily control the product, **but to be the prime source of the marketing materials!** That's it, in a nutshell. I've just given you the number one secret to selling successfully via direct marketing, especially information products.

When I first started selling information by mail, one of the first things I did was become a distributor for a line of books published by an outfit in California. The "distributor pack" they provided was quite good, with camera-ready sales materials for all the books. After copying and mailing thousands of circulars and letters with a very poor response, the obvious became clear to me. If I was just ONE distributor, how many others were mailing out the SAME materials to the same group of prospects? I decided to spend some time and create my own circulars and sales letters. The result? My sales increased by 30% and I was able to make some money selling books that were not originated by my company. This was a learning experience indeed.

However, many people fail because they do not spend the time or effort (or pay someone else) to come up with unique sales materials. For example, I was looking through one of the industry tabloids the other day, and there was a certain MLM program being advertised. It was one of those "monitored" programs with three names listed to whom you are to send money orders. Actually, it's really a pyramid but that's not the point. The point is that there were ten full-page ads for this very same program—*TEN!* The only difference was the names on the list. How successful do you think this ad will be? Well, maybe for the first one it might do OK, but how about the other nine? You don't have to be a genius to see that this is NOT the way to sell anything. The only winner in this case is the "monitor" who appears on every ad.

The same thing happens with most Multi-Level Marketing or dealership programs. You are given a set of ads, which is good, and asked to simply place your name and address on them. This works only if you are not placing ads in the same places as others promoting the same thing. If you are, you are just wasting your time. Successful promoters of MLM programs learn early on the value of developing unique marketing and promotional materials.

Furthermore, just because someone develops a product or program does NOT mean that they are necessarily a marketing expert. In other words, they might have a great product, but when it comes to marketing they couldn't sell peanuts to a starving elephant. You could sell a lot more of the product using your own materials than you ever could using the ones provided by the prime source.

A BETTER APPROACH

There are a few things you can do in order to successfully sell products that you don't produce. First of all, develop your OWN sales materials to sell the product. You should check with the prime source first for approval, but this will certainly help differentiate yourself from others selling the same thing. If you are placing ads, word the ads so that you do not necessarily mention the product by name. This way, people will respond to your ad, even though they may have already seen the product offered elsewhere. Once they respond, it's up to YOU to close the deal. Once again, this is done with killer sales materials. Honesty and integrity, along with strong customer service certainly help as well.

One other strategy is to purchase some quality reports or books with reprint rights. Depending on the limitations of the reprint rights, if any, you can then change the title and market it with your own materials. You might put three or four different booklets together and market it as a "system". Once again, the key is in the marketing. I know one very successful mail order operator who has done this many times over with great success. His strength is in writing advertising and marketing copy. It doesn't hurt that he has an aptitude for selecting quality information products. However, he never sells them under the original titles. He changes the titles, changes the content a bit and—voila! he's got his "own" product to sell.

Remember, in mail order it is not what you are selling, but HOW you sell it. Obviously I am not advocating you lie or deceive. I am referring to honest, yet creative and response-generating advertising and marketing. It's like your local grocery stores. Realistically, if you want a certain brand of product you could get it at any store in town. However, you shop at a certain store for one reason or another, usually as a result of that store's marketing. They may have better prices, service or promotions. The point is, they are all selling the same things, some just do a better job of marketing.

So don't get hung up about being the prime source for a product. If you spend your time honing your marketing and advertising skills you'll be able to take a product that's already out there and make a profit selling it. *They key is developing your OWN marketing materials.*

COMMISSION CIRCULARS-A WAY TO RICHES?

Almost every person in the mail order business gets involved with commission circular mailers. Like everything else, there are ways to make money by becoming a circular mailer. But, more often than not, you are going to lose money very quickly. I know of people who have had success with good circular mailing programs. However, I know of many more that nearly went broke chasing the riches promised by the promoters of worthless circular mailers.

For the uninformed, a Commission Circular Mailer is anyone who mails advertising flyers for a prime source, and receives a commission for orders received. The most popular commission circulars have a place for you to add your name in the "Send Order To" space in an advertising circular for a product or service someone else has developed. You then receive the orders, deduct your commission and send payment to the prime source, which then ships the order to your customer. Others have a number stamped on them, which identifies the mailer. The mailer receives commissions for all orders received with their number. Sounds easy, right? Well, the sad truth is that, except in rare cases, you will be lucky to recover your costs, much less turn a profit. The promoters stand a good chance to make money, because they use several people to mail out their programs, and save the cost of printing, postage, and mailing list costs. Plus, they usually charge you a registration fee for the "right" to sell their products, and for camera ready artwork, instructions, etc.

There are some people that have become rich by mailing commission circulars, and there are some honest promoters that have legitimate programs with a good chance of success. These are few and far between, but they are out there and if you find a good one, work it like crazy!

In order to profit from mailing circulars, the following qualities must be present in the program you are working:

The product must be a good one, with high sales appeal. It should be priced high enough to make you a profit, but low enough to attract buyers. Make sure it hasn't been sold to death over the years, and that there is still a demand. Also, it should not be readily available in stores or from other sources.

The prime source of the product must be reputable and dependable. You must know their name and telephone number so you can contact them. Be sure you are confident that they will fill your orders, and ship them on time.

The advertising circulars must be of high quality! They should be professionally designed and printed. The prime source should give you good camera-ready art, so that you can have the circulars reproduced with your name typeset. Or, they should supply you with preprinted, high quality circulars. Some companies may require you to order circulars directly from them. This can be a good thing, because they want to control the quality of the advertising circulars. On the other hand, some companies do this so that they can make money on the printing they sell you. Some companies may give you the option of ordering preprinted circulars from them, or printing them yourself. This is the best way, so that you can compare printing costs. In either case, ALWAYS USE HIGH QUALITY PRINTED CIRCULARS! Avoid using rubber stamps for your name and address inserts. It is always best to have these typeset to present a high quality image!

You must have access to a good mailing list! I'll cover mailing lists in more depth later on in this book. Just be sure that the list is a good one, and TEST IT FIRST! If you obtain names from the prime source, be sure that no two circular mailers will receive the same names!

One way to save on mailing costs is to find a reputable "Print And Mail" dealer who can mail the circulars for you. It is far cheaper than mailing them yourself, and a lot less work! Just be sure the dealer is reputable, and is sending out to a good list. As always, test a minimum amount before committing to a large mailing. You can also run your circular in one of the small tabloid type publications.

You should use circulars for generating repeat business from your own customers. This is mail order's biggest "secret" to being profitable-generate repeat business! Once you make a sale, quickly follow it up with a repeat offer for another product you are selling. This is where commission circulars can really work wonders. You already got the customer, and if they are satisfied, they will order from you again and again!

WANT THE REAL SUCCESS FOR MAIL ORDER?-SELL PICKS & PANS!

With the exception of established companies selling consumer products, there are two groups of people in mail order–those that are looking for a way to make money, and those that are providing them with the tools to do so. Rarely have I seen the former group make much money or build themselves a continuing business. However, the latter group is full of success stories. As one of my good mail order friends likes to say, "I make my money by selling picks & pans to the gold diggers".

LESSONS FROM THE GOLD RUSH

Let's go back a hundred and fifty years ago, to 1849. Oh yes, the great California Gold Rush. *"Go west young man, there's gold in them thar hills"* became a battle cry for so many that wanted to strike it rich. They came out to California in droves, seeking a quick fortune. For every one that actually discovered gold and staked a worthwhile working claim there were a thousand or more that made nothing. Families were destroyed and people were shot down in cold blood, all for a few dollars in gold or a worthless claim.

However, many savvy businessmen **DID** make a killing during the gold rush. They got rich all right, but not by digging for gold. **They got rich by selling all the gold prospectors the TOOLS to dig for the gold!** They realized that every one of those gold prospectors needed picks & pans and any number of other tools and resources to pursue their dreams. Many a "Gold Town" sprung up during that time, with the Livery Stables, Saloons, (and saloon "gals") Blacksmiths and General Store owners making a fortune. When the claims dried up so did the town. The smart entrepreneurs simply followed the prospectors to the next Gold Town.

The thought of selling "picks & pans" was nothing new and had been around since the days of the caveman. Yet it was never more apparent than the great gold rush days. Ever since, the successful entre-preneurs in this world usually got there by supplying "picks & pans" in one form or another. People wanted to get somewhere faster than horses? The automobile came along. Folks needed homes built? The construction industry started. Folks wanted to communicate easier? The telegraph, then the telephone came along. The list is endless. The point is, if you are looking to build a business that will allow you to work for yourself, your best bet is to sell TOOLS to those that are ALREADY IN BUSINESS or are seriously thinking about starting one. Stop looking for the one "program" or "system" that is going to make you rich. Instead, *try to find something that you can sell to people that are already in business!*

THE "PICKS & PANS" OF MAIL ORDER

Nowhere is this more evident than in mail order. Especially the business of selling INFORMATION by mail order. I talk to people all the time that are joining some new MLM company, or some "program" (99% of which are illegal pyramids or chains) or buying into some great new "secret" money making system in an effort to make their fortune, or "stake their claim" if you will. I have NEVER, in over 15 years of business, seen anybody build a continuing business by doing this. Oh sure, some make money, but not very much, or it's gone as fast as it came–just like those gold miners. The way to make money is to either be first, or be best. All the rest are simply pawns in the games played by the promoters.

However, I HAVE seen many an entrepreneur succeed by selling people the tools that they need to pursue these moneymaking plans. Think about the successful mail order companies. The ones that succeed provide useful products that fill a need to a particular market. No secret there, but it is tough to succeed and takes a lot of time and money to sell a catalog of products. Selling information is better, but it is the right information that matters. Tell people how to do something and you are filling a need. However, the companies that roll through all the different incarnations of mail order plans and programs are the ones selling the tools. Tools such as advertising, mailing lists, design and typesetting services, printing, postage services, commercial mailbox centers—you get the idea. The Internet is a great example of a modern day gold rush. Sure, some are making money by selling their products on the net. However, the BULK of the money is being made by service providers, web site designers, and others supplying the "tools" to doing business on the Internet.

When I first started in the information mail order business, I tried selling other people's moneymaking plans and ideas. Heck, it sounded so easy. If the promoter got rich by doing it, I figured that I could too. After all, I was smarter than them, with an MBA and business experience, right? Wrong. <u>Boy was I wrong</u>. I eventually started asking myself if these plans were so great, why were they selling me the information instead of doing it for themselves? Rarely did I find any of these promoters that were actually doing what they were selling. No, they were simply selling the tools.

THE "TOOLS" ARE ALREADY AVAILABLE FOR YOU TO SELL

If you are just starting out in mail order, or if you want to build a business that will succeed, concentrate on selling people "picks & pans". Contact mailing list companies and printers and ask to be a broker. Eventually, you can build your own in-house mailing lists through ads or other means and sell your own names. There is BIG money in doing this, believe me.

You can broker almost any service—advertising, designing, typesetting, you name it. Providers of these "tools" are always looking for new customers and will be more than happy to pay you a commission. Once you become accustomed to selling these types of products or services, you can then develop your own. This is where the real money is in mail order. You have to eventually become a prime source for something. Once you do that, you can continue to add more and more products or increase your customer base.

Remember, don't think in terms of trying to get rich quick in mail order. Take a look at what IS selling, and try to think of something that you can provide to all those hungry customers. Even the illegal pyramids have the right idea. The promoters provide the "tools" (the program, printing, etc.) to all those prospects. However, only the promoter or the very few people at the top make any money. Instead of looking for the next "gold rush" try selling people the "picks & pans". Mailing lists, printing and the myriad of mail order products and services will be around as long as people pursue mail order as a way to make money. They will all need tools to succeed, so it might as well be you that supplies them!

MARKETING YOUR PRODUCT

PRICING YOUR PRODUCT

The most important thing you need to do, once you decide what product or products you are going to sell is to determine a price. This is a difficult undertaking. Logic tells you to figure up all your expenses, including the cost of your product, overhead, marketing general administration fees, etc. and then add them up to arrive at the real price that product costs you. You then decide what your profit will be and that is your selling price. This works fine with tangible products, but not with informational products.

The biggest expense you will have, other than the acquisition cost if you are buying the product is your advertising and marketing expense. This is why you need a much larger mark up in mail order than many other businesses, you've got to cover that advertising and marketing nut. A good rule of thumb when selling products is to sell the item for 5 times what it costs you. In other words, if you pay $5 for a product you should sell it for $25. Once again, this does not always work for information because with information you are many times selling a "perceived" value as opposed to the actual "cost" of producing your information product.

Basically, the price you should sell at is whatever the market will bear. Test your product at different price levels to see which one generates the most profits for you. For a book, anywhere from $14.95 to $29.95 is common.

Be sure that you also account for any shipping costs. Just be careful you are not selling products too cheaply–remember, you MUST make a profit after all is said and done.

DRAWING CUSTOMERS INTO YOUR MAIL ORDER "STORE"

It's no secret that the key to success in retail is to get people into the store. The same principals apply to mail order. Of course you don't have a physical store that customers can visit. Instead, you have a catalog or stable of products that you offer. It doesn't matter if you have a huge store or a simple catalog, if you don't get people to visit your business you will never succeed.

Retail stores have this practice down to a science, literally. How often do you see huge ads for things like soda, beer or snack items? Are the stores making huge profits by selling these products so cheaply? Of course not. In fact, many times they are actually LOSING money on the sale of these products. The only reason that they offer them for such a low price is to lead you into the store. Hence the term "loss leader", which means that they offer a highly saleable product in huge demand at a loss in order to "lead" you into the store with the intention of selling you other products on which they DO make a profit. Auto Parts stores are famous for this practice with motor oil. Many times they will offer sales of motor oil at a loss in order to entice you into their particular store instead of the competition. Once you are in the store, they sell you filters, tools and any other number of products. These are the "back end" sales of the retail trade.

Another tactic stores use, once they draw you in, is to place items that are the most popular in the back of the store. Ever notice that the items you use everyday, such as milk, orange juice, meats and the like are located in the BACK of the store? This is not by accident. It's done so that you have to walk down all those aisles of products just begging for a piece of your hard-earned money.

APPLYING THE PRINCIPALS TO MAIL ORDER

If you're selling something by direct mail, you need to attract potential customers. This is the number one priority. After all, if you don't first attract "potential" customers, how in the world can you expect to make any sales? You can use the same strategies that retail stores use to not only attract prospects, but keep them as well. Don't make the mistake of trying to sell your products on the front end unless you can afford to place a lot of full-page ads. Even with full-page ads, it is much more effective to place ads that "draw" customers to your company. If they are happy with what you give them on the INITIAL contact, there's a good chance that they're going to buy more products from you. The trick is to get the initial contact, and make it be in such a way that you qualify your prospect. In other words, you want them to be interested in what you are offering on the back end as well as the front end. An auto parts store does not lead you into the store with a sale on motor oil to sell you shoes. You shouldn't offer something on the front end that doesn't strongly relate to what you sell on the back end.

Some people make the mistake of thinking that once they get a prospect they can sell them anything. This type of thinking will lose you a lot of money in advertising. For example, if you are selling "how to" books on making money, don't lure prospects with a generic "FREE INFORMATION" ad promising great riches unless your information actually shows them how to earn money, and is not simply a bunch of unrelated "get-rich-quick" offers.

There are many ways to lure customers to your mail order "store". You can use free offers, premiums, special sales or other incentives. One of the most effective ways is to use a loss leader on the front end to get people to actually purchase something from you. Give them value for their money, and they'll be back for more.

THE SECRET OF SUCCESSFUL FRONT-END OFFERS

Well get into advertising a little later on, but I want to touch on it briefly here. Like most mail order people, I started out trying to sell one main product from a classified ad. Didn't work. Then I tried the "two-step" method by placing a classified asking for a SASE or a small fee for information. Worked a little better, but still not good enough. Then I went the *"FREE INFORMATION"* route and placed ads offering free information. This worked much better, but I wasn't getting many sales. In other words, people were answering my ad, but only because they wanted the free stuff. Even though I was following up with a strong sales package, I wasn't qualifying my customers.

Then I stumbled upon the secret. I started placing an ad for a small booklet related to my product. I didn't give this booklet away; I charged a couple bucks. I also made sure that I filled these orders with a booklet that had a much higher perceived value than the purchase price. **BINGO**! Suddenly I was not only pulling in some orders from my initial ad, but I was turning those prospects into customers on the back end as well. I didn't even care if the initial ad made money. I just wanted to draw enough prospects into my "store" to make a profit on the follow up sales.

You can do this too! It is not difficult and you'll find your sales increasing at an eye-popping rate. For example, let's say that you are trying to sell a book on home gardening for $19.95. That's a little too much to sell from a small display ad and not enough to sell via direct marketing. Even if you had a $17.00 gross profit, you'd still have to get a 2% response just to cover your postage. You could offer free information, but you would receive a lot of responses for people that were not really interested in what you are selling. However, you can offer a small report or booklet with "101 Gardening Tips" for $2 or $3 and sell it from a one or two-inch display ad. Now you will get people sending for your booklet that are actually interested in gardening. Fill the order with a professionally printed booklet (you can get a 12 page booklet printed for about 12¢ that will have a perceived value of more than $5.00) and your sales package for the gardening book or a catalog of other books. You are using the small ad to "draw customers to your store".

This is just one example of using a strong, inexpensive front-end offer to draw customers to your company. As you get better at writing ads, and more financially secure, you can even offer free information. Just be sure that you are qualifying your prospects so that you are offering something related to the rest of your products.

Once you draw customers to your "store" don't forget to lead them through the "aisles" of your catalog, just like a retail store. Place the most popular sellers inside the catalog so that the customer has to page through the rest of the catalog, looking at as many of your products as possible. You may mention the best seller on the cover, with a "See Page…". The point is that you want to expose your prospect to as many items in your catalog as possible to maximize your potential sale. Whatever you do, make sure that your customer is satisfied so that they keep coming back!

DIRECT MARKETING IS EASY–IT REALLY IS!

Now before you think I've hit my head one too many times and gone completely off kilter, bear with me. Direct Marketing, like many other aspects of business, is really not as difficult as it seems.

I once had a basketball coach in high school, some 20+ years ago now *(yikes!)* who admonished us when we would play poorly. "It's a ****&&%%$$##** easy game!", he would shout. "All you have to do is dribble the ball, pass the ball, and put the ball in the little round hole!" We got a kick out of watching this portly caricature with the bad toupee telling us that basketball was easy. Just once I wanted to see him get out there and try it. But you know something? He was onto something!

See, before there was Michael Jordan, there was a pretty spectacular player named Julius Erving, or "Dr. J" as he was called. He had more moves than former President Bill Clinton on an intern and all the kids wanted to be like Dr. J. Invariably, a guy *(could've even been me a time or two!)* would streak down the court for an easy lay up, and for some unknown reason suddenly think he was Dr. J. Instead of simply putting the ball in the basket, he would try some fancy behind the back slam-dunk move, and, more often than not, miss the shot! This would cause our coach to go nuts! *"It's an easy game! Stop trying to impress people and make it difficult."* I can still hear those words ringing in my ears!

Which, finally, brings me to the point I want to make. Direct Mail is, in it's simplest form, easy. You simply identify a target market, find an unfulfilled need, develop or locate a product to fill that need, and BOOM! You have it made!

Of course it's not quite that simple, but so many times people try to impress themselves or, worse, their customers and make things much more difficult than they have to be. The greatest sales people in the world will tell you that it's easy to sell when you believe in your product. This is why so many people selling rip-off schemes or products of little value rarely succeed. They simply cannot get behind the product and make people believe that the product will help them. My Dad was a great salesman and he once told me *"it's easy to sell something you believe in and would use yourself"*. So, first and foremost, make sure that you truly believe in what you're trying to sell.

YOU MUST GET BACK-END SALES

Once you sell a customer a product or service that fills a particular need, you need to keep that customer alive! Don't let him or her buy from you once and then disappear. How do you do this? First of all by treating them fairly from the beginning, and letting them know that you care about them. Make customer service your second priority, a close second to providing a quality product or service. Once they buy from you, they will trust you and will buy other products. You *must* have other products or services to sell to them or you will not keep that customer. So, develop a complete product line so that you can continue selling existing customers.

Give your customer a reason to trust you and believe in your company. Whatever you do, make sure you maintain a level of integrity and honesty. I recall one time I was sitting in on a presentation to an eager buyer with one of my sales reps for my import company. The buyer wanted to purchase one of the products we were importing at the time, with which we had some potential problems. It would have been a huge sale. Many salesmen would have made the sale, regardless of the potential problems down the road. However, the sales rep convinced the buyer that the products were not right for him, and walked away without an order. I was impressed at his honesty and asked him why he didn't just make the sale. He replied, *"Because I can't shave in the dark."* "What?" I asked. He explained that he had to look at himself in the mirror each morning and if he made that sale he could not have done it because he knew the potential problems that would arise. Aha, I said to myself, *"integrity"*. To this day I have no problem looking in the mirror. Make sure you don't either.

START WITH PROVEN PRODUCTS

You don't have to reinvent the wheel. There are products available that you can start selling right now. The best to start with are items that a majority of people need, and which they will use up and buy again. Examples are mailing lists, printing services, labels or rubber stamps, typesetting services, etc. Hook up with a reputable provider of these services and become a distributor or broker for them. You can start out with very little investment and make decent profits. Best of all, you are building a customer base which will order from you again and again.

DEVELOP YOUR OWN PRODUCT LINE

Eventually, if you intend to fully succeed in direct marketing, you must develop your own line of products. You then develop a network of distributors and dealers to sell these products for you. This is using "leverage" to market your products. You make less profit per sale, but you have a much greater marketing exposure without high costs of advertising and marketing, which are the responsibility of the dealers and distributors. It is at this point that you can really start to make some big bucks!

TEST, TEST, TEST!

Very few people make a huge income right from the start. You have to continue learning and testing different variables. There is no way around this, and it is a simple concept. If something is not working, change it a little. Test different variables of your ads, prices, guarantees, etc. More importantly, measure your results so you can see what changes bring in more sales and profits.

TWO KEYS TO PROFITABLE NETWORK MARKETING AND MAIL ORDER

Contrary to what many people may tell you, it IS possible to make a good living from network marketing and/or mail order. First of all, it is important to understand that neither of these is a "business" in itself. Instead, they are both methods of selling and distribution.

With that understood, the two keys to succeeding are to either be a great sales person OR find someone else to sell for you. That's it, in a nutshell. If you are in business, you are selling something. If it's not face-to-face then it is via direct mail, telephone, the Internet or some other means, but you MUST sell or you certainly cannot make money.

Which brings us to our two methods of succeeding. I've always contended that the real heavy-hitters in network marketing are successful because they are natural sales people. They hold meetings, conduct seminars and generally try to sell their products to every person they come in contact with. The same is true for direct mail. Think of the great pitchman you see on TV, like Don LaPree or Matthew Lesko. Remember Tony Little or Susan powder? One thing that they all have in common is that they are great pitchmen. Regardless of how irritating or full of boloney they appear, they move products! If you like selling you only need to find products to market and that is the easy part, as I've written about many times. Products are everywhere.

However, most of us don't like to sell, at least not on a personal level. So, what can we do? Find someone to sell for you. This is where dealer networks and independent sales reps come in. Face it, in business you are either the source of your own products or you are trying to sell someone else's product. Being the source of the product does NOT necessarily mean that you are the actual manufacturer or producer. It simply means that you control the marketing of the product under your company's banner. For example, Sears does not MAKE anything, yet they sell a lot of different products under the Sears name. In mail order, it's the same idea. If you do not control products as the source you are, in essence, selling products for someone else. Believe me, you do NOT have to be the "prime source" to make money in mail order.

Why do companies need dealers, or independent sales people? Well, if you read what many say it's because they want to make ALL the money and have you do ALL the work and marketing. Sure, many scam companies do this. However, there are other companies that utilize dealers for strictly ethical business purposes and it's a win/win situation. They really do "most" of the work and use the dealers to generate leads or customers as a source of leverage. Most people who complain that the prime source makes all the money while the dealers do all the work and bear all the expense are ignorant about how products are sold, plain and simple. Or, they are dealers that don't do what they are supposed to do–SELL! So they whine about the prime source ripping them off. Look, if you are going to be a dealer, you are going to have to sell–either in person or via direct marketing. One point I'd like to make here is that we <u>ALL</u> have the opportunity to become a prime source. If you are not willing to do it, don't blame those that are.

Let me give you a real-life example of how sales reps work, and why they are used. A few years ago my company represented a Taiwan manufacturer of car covers. They wanted a U.S. operation, so we set it up and managed it for them. Now came the hard part—marketing the covers. In the automotive aftermarket, as in most industries, there are sales agencies called "manufacturer's representative firms" that do just that–they represent many different manufacturers in a certain industry. They control a certain geographical territory and service all of the customers in that territory. They do all the selling, working with the manufacturer or "source" of the product. For their efforts, they receive a commission on all sales. Most reps have a dominant product line they represent and other related products.

We could have hired in-house sales people in all the different territories to sell the car covers. Then, we would have had to pay them salaries and benefits and absorbed all the headaches and overhead of having employees. They would get paid whether they made any sales or not! Then, we'd have to pay all the travel and marketing expenses. How many people would we need to hire to cover the whole country? Fifty? A hundred? A thousand? As a small start-up company this was not feasible. So, I hired <u>nine</u> manufacturer's rep firms that covered <u>all</u> <u>fifty states</u>. They all had their own sales people and absorbed their own marketing and operating expenses. We provided them with samples, marketing materials and support. It was a win/win situation, as it should be. This is how most consumer products are sold today, through independent sales people.

The same concepts hold true in mail order. ***It's called getting the maximum sales leverage for the least amount of money.*** To do this, you need to have dealers selling your products. Now I am NOT talking about scams like envelope stuffing or "work-at-home" opportunities. Use your head; nobody is going to pay you $1 to "stuff" an envelope to mail for them when they can have a mail house do it for pennies.

However, as a dealer you CAN make money, IF you deal with reputable companies and IF you are willing to learn how to market and sell. The more people a company has marketing for them, the more coverage or leverage they have. Can you blame a company for trying to maximize its marketing efforts while minimizing the costs? Once again, it must be a win/win situation between the dealer and the prime source. The dealer sells, the prime source helps them sell and gives them the tools and support needed. The dealer makes a commission, from which expenses are deducted. This is the dealer's profit. The prime source bears the costs of production, marketing, fulfillment, order processing, shipping and other expenses. So they certainly don't make ALL the money, as some would have you believe.

So ask yourself—are you a seller, or do you want to market a product and have people sell it for you? Of course many mail order companies are both. Heck, we have numerous products that we actually produce ourselves. We also have others that we purchase from outside sources or sell as a dealer. We also use dealers to sell many of our products as well as pushing them on our own. We could NEVER cover the whole market by ourselves, and our dealers help us. For their efforts, they are paid commissions and given a lot of support.

You can make money as a dealer, but you need several related products and at least one dominant product that you sell. Preferably, you should have at least ONE product you can control as the source and sell it as your lead product.

Look at any successful mail order company in the "how to" market and you'll find they either use dealers for marketing leverage or have grown to a point where they can afford to do it all themselves. Remember my friend, it's all about *leverage!*

CREATING EFFECTIVE MARKETING MATERIALS

In mail order, the most important part of your sales effort, aside from your customer list, is the quality of your sales literature. Since it is the only vehicle you have to attract customers, it should be of top quality! Nothing will turn off a potential customer faster than poorly written, or poorly printed literature.

I cannot believe some of the pieces we receive in the mail. Many times, the flyer or brochure is so badly printed that it is almost illegible. Other times, it is quite clear that the flyer or brochure has been photocopied many times over, with poor quality printing or paper. Why do people waste their money with these poor sales materials? Well, take a look at what the poorly printed or written flyers are selling. Usually it is some chain letter, envelope stuffing, or bogus MLM scheme. These are not legitimate mail order dealers, and they are lazy! They are after the quick bucks, and do not take any time or effort to create a sales piece that will attract buyers! Usually, these people try one program, photocopy a couple hundred or so flyers, and mail them out, expecting to rake in huge profits! Well, those of us that have been around awhile know that this does not happen, so these people have just wasted their money! It is just as well, because it is one more bogus dealer that the legitimate mail order dealers have to deal with.

Getting high quality written literature involves much more than just finding a good printer. First of all, you must take a good look at the content of the flyer itself. Is it well written? Is it to the point? Does it clearly indicate exactly what it is you are selling, the pricing, and all pertinent information? Be sure that all spelling, punctuation, and grammar are correct *BEFORE YOU EVEN THINK ABOUT GETTING IT PRINTED!* If you are making your own flyer, be sure you have the skills to make it a good one. If not, and you truly believe in the product you are selling, then spend some money to have a professional create a powerful flyer for you. You can find the names of many people offer typesetting and copywriting services by looking through many of the business opportunity and mail order publications. You will see many ads for these services. Or, look in your phone book under "Graphic artists" or "Desktop Publishing" services.

OK, so you have your flyer, and are confident it is a good one. You have read, reread, and reread it to be sure there are no spelling, punctuation or grammar errors. Now, you are ready to prepare the piece for printing. First of all, remember that *YOU MUST START WITH A GOOD, CLEAN ORIGINAL.* This is usually referred to as a "camera ready" master in the trade. Everything is based on the original that you present for printing. When you get it printed, whether it be on a copy machine or printing press, the final result is dependent upon the original you present for duplication. If your original is dirty or contaminated in any way it will only be magnified when it is printed. The camera truly sees everything, so provide crisp, clean originals or you will not be happy.

In order to supply good originals, always use a good quality paper stock (24# bright white coated paper is best) and be sure it is white, no matter what the final color of the product will be. Always give your printer an original document, not a photocopy. If you use a computer to produce your original, be sure to use a Laser printer with a resolution of at least 600 DPI. 1200 DPI is much better and preferable. Stay away from dot matrix printers, which produce ragged text and graphics. If you really want high quality, have your original produced on an ultra-high resolution printer found at many local printing service outlets. These resolutions start at 1,200 DPI and are especially good for documents that contain graphics or photographs. If you do use photographs, make sure to have them "screened" first.

Do not use typewriters. If you cannot do quality work yourself, pay to have it done right! Also, do not use paper clips, staples, tape, or fold your originals. All of these will leave telltale signs that will be picked up during duplication.

Next you need to find the "RIGHT" printer. Most quick print shops do OK work, and are good for smaller quantities. But, if you are going to have more than a thousand copies made, you are better off using a printer that can do Offset Printing. SHOP AROUND! Printers vary greatly in price, service, and quality. The most expensive is not always the best. If you can afford to wait a little while for your job, mail order printers can be very inexpensive. Just be sure to use a reputable one, which guarantees its work!!

Paper color is also important. Color paper is much cheaper than using colored ink and can be just as effective. Be sure to use a good quality paper (20# Bond is best), and avoid harsh color combinations, like red ink on dark blue paper. You want the flyer to look good, and invite reading! Remember, no matter how good the printed product looks, it is of no value if it never gets read. Never try to squeeze your work into too small an area. Use as much space as necessary, and avoid overusing fonts or graphics. While these can be very effective, too much of them is a turn off.

One other note, if you are using a camera-ready original which you are just adding your name and address, have it typeset! A rubber stamp imprint is not nearly as effective and looks sloppy and amateurish. Never, ever hand write your name and address on a circular! The point is, you want to create a good impression, and come across as a professional mail order operator. By using high quality materials, and clear, crisp printing, you can make a good impression. *And remember, you never get a second chance to make a good first impression!*

LOW COST AND NO-COST MARKETING STRATEGIES

There are some great low cost and no cost methods for distributing your circulars, flyers, and other sales material. These methods can be very effective, and, more importantly, give you increased coverage at very little cost. When you consider that it costs $340.00 to mail out 1,000 pieces of your marketing materials via First Class mail at current rates, the cost savings realized from these alternate distribution methods will enable you to invest more money in your advertising and marketing programs.

First of all, understand that Direct Mailing to a specified list (providing that the list is a GOOD one) is still the fastest way to promote your offer. However, you will spend a lot of money mailing to these lists, and the good lists are expensive. Furthermore, you are mailing to people already in the business, or those that have a specific interest in your product. This is beneficial and productive, and should be done using the best list you can afford. But, there are so many people out there that would be interested in your offers, if only they could be reached. These potential customers are not on any list, because they have not yet started to answer opportunity ads, or send for offers via the mail that would get their names put on such lists. They are great prospects; they just do not know it yet!!

How do you reach these neophytes? You could mail to a random list pulled from anywhere, but this is expensive and waste of time. So, you distribute your material right in your own community, at a fraction of what it would cost you to mail it. There are many potential customers right in your area, that are just waiting to respond to your offers-you just have to get that offer to them.

First of all, you can distribute the flyers directly to the homes of potential customers. Hire teenagers or others looking for part time work to put your circulars or flyers on doors, car windshields, or handouts at local businesses. Remember though, it is illegal to put ANYTHING in a private mailbox unless it has been mailed. So, do not insert in mailboxes or you are asking for trouble from the U.S. Postal Service. Try to distribute your materials at apartment and condominium complexes, working class housing developments, and parking lots of malls and other areas frequented by the "average Person". These places all contain excellent potential customers, and allow for several hundred or thousand flyers to be distributed in a short period of time. The idea is to try and distribute the sales material as efficiently as possible. You will be reaching many new potential customers.

Next, visit local businesses that are frequented by your potential target market. These may include Laundromats, restaurants, supermarkets, barbershops, arcades, etc. Anywhere that large groups of people frequent or assemble. Simply place batches of your brochures or flyers in these places with a card or note that says, "FREE-TAKE ONE". You can get a little more elaborate here and make up some nice holders from cardboard, or buy plastic ones. You can even make a nice Point Of Purchase (POP) display to entice people to pick up your brochures and/or flyers. The point is, people will take them, read them, and many may actually respond. Be sure that you check with the proprietors of these businesses and get their permission to leave your materials, if necessary. This method of distribution requires some patience and time. But, once you have an established group of outlets for your brochures it becomes a set route. Just replenish your materials as they are depleted and treat it seriously. This method produces VERY good results if your offer is appealing. Look to set up from 20-40 outlets around your community.

Another method that works is hooking up with any number of businesses that deliver products to their customers. The best are pizza places, or similar types of delivery services. Simply have the delivery person leave your sales flyer with each customer to which they deliver. The people tend to "read" when they eat, and you have just provided them with some reading material!

As an added incentive to get local businesses to work with you, you can give them a commission for orders received from the flyers placed at their location or delivered with their products. Just code each order form for the specific business, and credit them when orders are received. Many businesses will be more than happy to cooperate with you.

Finally, you can place ads in the "Free" or low cost shopping guides, newspapers and other publications. Ask the respondents to send you a SASE and mail them your offer. One thing I suggest when offering mail order opportunities in your local community is to use a P.O. Box.

Unless you have a business location separate from your home this is a necessity. You do not want people showing up at your house, and a P.O. Box will help you avoid this.

HOW TO CREATE AN ENDLESS FLOW OF QUALITY PROSPECTS FOR JUST A FEW DOLLARS A WEEK!

You can easily generate an endless list of qualified prospects for your mail order business for just a few dollars a week. Unlike expensive mailing lists you, these prospects are more qualified and they are yours to use for FREE! Here's how you do it:

First of all, you use a strategy which we call "reverse mailing". A "reverse" or "bounce back" mailing simply means that you mail your mailing list offer back to people that have sent you an offer in the mail similar to what you are selling or promoting. Doing reverse mailings is perhaps the most cost effective method for generating quality leads. The best part about it is that you don't need to spend a lot of money to use this strategy, and you are guaranteed of receiving highly qualified prospects that are proven to purchase opportunities similar to yours.

I have not purchased a mailing list for my own direct mailings in years–haven't had to. Yet, I've built an in-house list of thousands and thousands of names through different methods that have been successful for me. Once you build a list such as we have, there are additional profits to be realized by renting that list–but that is the topic of a future book on how to actually compile and rent mailing lists. To learn how to profit and earn a huge income as a list broker, purchase my book **HOW TO EARN A HUGE INCOME FROM HOME SELLING MAILING LISTS**. It is available directly from TJT Publications, PO Box 55685, Valencia, CA 91385. Or, call 661-291-2353 or fax 661-291-2354 for more information.

The first thing you need to do in order to successfully use reverse mailings is to get people mailing their offers to you. This takes a little bit of time and effort, but before too long you will end up with a steady flow of "junk mail" coming to your mailbox. This will certainly not be junk mail to you–it will be worth its weight in gold because these are your potential customers!

So, how do you create this flow of junk mail? There are a few different methods. The first, and most popular (although not necessarily the best) is to write to every mailing list company you can find promoting business or money-making opportunity names. You want to get put on their list. However, if you just say "put me on your list" most companies promoting quality lists won't do it. They are selling names that they hope respond to their customer's offers. They do not want a bunch of names that are only interested in getting mail sent to them. However, the cheaper quality mailing lists will list you–and this is what you want.

A better way is to write the company and just ask for their price list or more information about their mailing lists. Or, you can say you are promoting a mail order or MLM program and you would like to receive information about their mailing lists. You can also request to be put on their list to receive other offers. Most companies are so desperate for fresh names that they'll put you on the list. Now, you need to write the same companies over and over again–every three months or so, so that your name stays on the mailing list company's active rental list. Otherwise, as your name gets older it will be purged from the list (although many of the cheap quality mailing list companies will keep a name forever–as long as it is deliverable). You can also get your name listed in many different ways with the same mailing list company–use your street address and your P.O. Box, change your first name, etc.–the point is that you want your name to get rented as many times as possible. You WANT more and more junk mail!

Once you are listed, your name will be rented to many people that are promoting different programs, books, opportunities, etc. When you receive these offers, you do your reverse mailing to them for your mailing lists. These are excellent prospects, as I've said, because you

KNOW they are looking for new ways to make money. It might as well be from YOUR program!

Another strategy to get your name on mailing lists is to start answering ads and purchasing products from the mail order publications. That's right–you've got to spend a little, although not a lot. Buy some of the programs or systems you see advertised. As you purchase these products, you're name will certainly be sold to mailing list companies, or rented to others. Many of these lists will tend to be a little more "professional" so you will get offers from people that are actually serious about mail order. Hence, they will be better prospects for your MLM program, and will recognize the value of the quality program you are offering. For example, if you buy one of the systems advertised on the infomercials, you can bet your name will be quickly rented or sold to numerous mailing list companies, resulting in an endless flow of "offers" in your mailbox.

You should answer as many ads as you possibly can–both the FREE information ads as well as the ones asking for a nominal fee. Once again, these companies will sell your name to others. This process takes time, so keep at it. In about 30-60 days you'll start to see the offers coming in trying to sell you everything under the sun. You are not interested in what they are trying to sell YOU. You want them to know what you can sell THEM. Never again will you be upset about all that "junk mail" filling your mailbox. You'll realize that all these "gold diggers" are looking for a way to make money–and you are going to be more than happy to provide them that opportunity!

The key to using reverse mailings is to generate as many potential prospects as you possibly can. You want to try to get to a point where you are doing 50 reverse mailings a day–or more. If you want to save some money on mailing, you can use postcards. We GIVE you the postcards to use, and they work! Plus, they only cost you 20¢ to mail, as opposed to 34¢ for a First Class letter.

When you start receiving your coveted "junk mail" there are some pieces that you should disregard. You need to check the return address to make sure that the person or company promoting the piece of mail is actually the one that mailed it to you. For example, many MLM and dealership programs use company provided marketing materials, with the actual prime source's address listed. This is usually indicated by a "code number," a "department or suite number" or some other indication that tells you the mailing was sent by an independent dealer or distributor.

You do not want to waste your time mailing your information back to these companies because it will go to the "prime source", and not to the dealer or distributor that actually mailed you the materials. As I said, the easiest way to tell is to check the postmark against the return address. If they are different cities or states, you will not have the actual address of the mailer. You can also tell if you start receiving a lot of the same postcards, letters or fliers with different codes or departments.

By using the strategies I've shown you above, you will soon be generating more leads than you'll know what to do with. Send your offers to these names–and send them more than once! Repetition is a great marketing tool. These prospects cost you next to nothing, yet they are much more responsive and qualified than any list you can rent! Remember, keep at it. Prospecting by mail is a numbers game–the more numbers you generate, the more successful you'll be!

SHOULD YOU GET AN 800 # FOR YOUR BUSINESS?

It's no secret that an 800 number makes it more convenient for your customers to contact you. Notice I said more *convenient*, not *easier*. The real reason for an 800 number is to say to your customer "call us, we'll even pay for the call". This immediately takes away a barrier to getting that customer to call. But do you really NEED an 800 number to be successful? No, you don't. More importantly, if you do decide to use an 800 number you have to make sure that it does not end up being counter-productive to your profit margins.

Many so called "marketing experts" will tell you that you must have an 800 number. That's all fine and good, except that they are *NOT* paying for your 800 number! Just because everyone seems to be getting an 800 number does NOT mean that you need one. Like Mom used to say, "If all of your friends jumped off a bridge, would you?" I used to think; well yeah I might, depending on what was at the bottom! But that's another story. Let's get back on track here.

First the positives. Having an 800 number makes it easier for your customers to order, as I've stated. It also makes you look like a "real company" in the eyes of a customer. They will automatically think you must be successful because, after all, you have your own 800 number! This is not necessarily true anymore. See, years ago an 800 number (or WATS line as they were called) was an expensive undertaking. You needed a dedicated number, paid a substantial set up fee, and incurred hefty monthly charges. You then had to pay for the calls into your 800 number, at high long-distance rates. However, with deregulation came more phone companies, better technology, and reduced long-distance rates. Now you can get an 800 number from any number of providers, and you don't need a separate phone line. The 800 number is simply connected to your normal number. The set-up charges are low, or free, and there are usually no other monthly fees. In a nutshell, getting an 800 number is easy. That's not the problem.

YOU MUST ACCOUNT FOR THE COST OF YOUR 800#

The problem comes when you have an 800 number, and you don't have the sales to support it. Or, worse yet, you don't build the cost of the number into your prices. Like anything else you offer a customer, you have to account for it in your cost of sales. You really don't think companies "give" you anything do you? Of course not. Advertising, marketing, promotions and premiums are all built into the sales price. So, if you offer an 800 number, be sure that your sales prices reflect this cost! For example, let's say you have a product that sells for $20. To make it simple, let's say you pay 10¢ per minute for your 800 number, and each call for an order averages 5 minutes. So, the cost of taking that call is 50¢. That is 2.5% of your sales price! So, you must be sure that you build that 2.5% into your cost of sales. If you only sell a product for $10, suddenly that call is 5% of your sales price! So, you must have the margins to support the 800 number and you must account for it!

An 800# Can Eat Up Your Profits In A Hurry

Let's assume you do have the sales to support your 800 number. Now comes the REAL problem. What about the customers that call the 800 number but don't order? Maybe they are calling for information, customer service, or just to chat! You are throwing money away! I talked to one gentleman not too long ago that was spending over $65,000 a year for his 800 number. He estimated that $20,000 of that was NOT related to orders! That's a lot of cabbage to throw away every year! So, what do you do?

One thing you can do is state that your 800 number is for "orders only". On your sales literature, clearly indicate that the 800 number is for orders. Give another number for customer service or general information. This way you are only paying for calls that are definite orders. If you do this, you should have a separate line for your 800 number so you can tell if a call is coming in on your 800 line or regular phone number. If you have the 800 number tied to your regular number; there is no way to tell. Make sure you nicely enforce the "orders only" rule.

Will You Really Benefit From An 800 Number?

There are many major mail order companies that do not offer an 800 number. However, they usually offer unique products, or their products are much less expensive than other companies. If your product or service is unique enough, people will call you no matter what if they want what you offer. For example, we sell custom automotive floor mats via mail order (*Call IMC, Inc. (805) 291-1289 if you need a set!*).

We do NOT offer an 800 number. We tried one once, but found that it did not increase our sales. Why? Because the items are custom made, very unique, and priced 30-50% below retail. In this case, if the customer is looking for custom mats they are not going to care if it's a toll call.

TEST, TEST, TEST

You knew I was going to say this, didn't you? Like anything else in direct marketing, you must test! You might send out half of your catalogs with your 800 number and half without. Code them and see if there is a noticeable difference in response. Test using an 800 number for orders and a toll number for customer service. By doing this you can see if the cost of using an 800 number is justified, or if the money should be better used for other marketing efforts.

An 800 number is a nice thing to have, but not if it ends up COSTING you profits! If you want one, be sure it will increase your sales and make certain you account for the cost in your sales prices! If you cannot, you're better off without one!

THE SECRET OF PERCEIVED VALUE (AS OPPOSED TO "DECEIVED" VALUE)

One of the first things you'll learn marketing information via mail order is that the actual "value" of what you are selling is of much less importance than what your customers *think* the information is worth. This is what we call "perceived value"–how much value your customers place on something, not the actual cost. You might sell a book that cost you $20 to produce, but if it doesn't benefit the customer in a way that he or she feels they got their twenty bucks worth you are going to have an unhappy customer. On the other hand, you could produce a book for under a buck that will make your customer feel as if it's worth more than the $20 book, providing the information is perceived as such.

This is the beauty of selling information, the huge profits possible because of perceived value.

However, there is a fine line between perceived value and "deceived value" as I like to call it. Many customers already have a prejudice toward mail order sellers, particularly when it relates to "how to" or business opportunity information. Because of this, we as sellers must constantly come up with new marketing and advertising angles in order to get the leery customer to respond. Once they do, you better give them something worthwhile or they are not likely to buy anything from you again. Nothing will tick off a customer faster than receiving something which makes them feel as if they were deceived. Yet this is exactly what many mail order sellers do. They write a great sales letter or circular and then provide a product which is nothing more than a poorly veiled attempt to get the customer to buy into something else. There is NOTHING wrong with trying to bump a customer into another, more expensive product. In fact, it is a necessary sales strategy in mail order. However, the FIRST product must be perceived as having value on it's own. If it does not, your customer will feel as if they've been conned and this is NOT what you want!

Perceived value plays a huge role in premiums or special "FREE" bonuses you give as enticements for your customers to buy. If you are selling information by mail order, it is imperative that you give something as a freebie in order to wet your customer's whistle a little bit. Just look at magazine publishers, like Sports Illustrated. They give a free video, basketball, jacket, sweatshirt or SOMETHING that has a high-perceived value. People subscribe just to get the free bonus and not necessarily for the subscription. However, once they subscribe it is hoped that they will continue to subscribe.

In mail order the secret is not *what* you initially sell a customer. The key is that they buy ANYTHING from you and are satisfied. Then you can sell them more and more "backend" products. This is where your real profits come from. When selling information, offering a free bonus works much better than offering a discount, no matter what anybody tries to tell you. However, the bonus needs to have a high-perceived value so that your customer feels they are really getting something special. Just as importantly, it must cost you very little so that you can provide the bonus without raising the price of your product by too much. The fact is, the "free" bonus is certainly figured into the cost of your product. This means that the lower it costs you, the more competitive you can price your product. This is all relative to the price of your product. If you are selling a book for $20 and want to add a free bonus you certainly don't want to add a bonus that costs you $10. This would mean that your product would now have to be priced at over $30 just to cover the bonus. However, if your product is selling for over $100, now that $10 cost for the premium is not so bad.

I can't stress it enough; the key is to give your customer a bonus that has a high-perceived value. So, what can you offer as a freebie that has a high perceived value but little cost? Free reports are good as they can be obtained or written by yourself easily and reproduced for pennies. However, the free report angle is overused and is most effective for products selling for under $10 or so. Also, be sure the report is really a "report" and not just a sales circular trying to sell the customer something else. Of course you want to include as many backend offers as possible, but don't call these the "Free Report". Do this and you've just crossed the line from perceived value to deceived value.

If you really want to give your customers worthwhile bonuses with high-perceived value, try cassette tapes. You can duplicate tapes in lots of just a couple hundred for about 75¢ each. Yet, everybody knows tapes are "worth" about $10-$15. CD's are good, as are diskettes containing information or software of some sort. Books are another great free bonus, especially if you call them a "system" or "course" or something other than just a plain old book.

Information is a funny thing. It really has NO value unless it's used and implemented. Too often I see people trying to beef up a book or package by increasing the page count by using large type face, a lot of graphics, etc. This is fine and is a good tactic to use, providing you are still giving the customer what they paid for as far as content is concerned. People seem to place a higher value on quantity over quality, and this is a dilemma you face when selling information. People who really see the VALUE in the information and USE it want as much as you can give them, no matter the size. Give them a bunch of fluff and filler and you've deceived them.

Over the years there have been many classic examples of great advertising promoting deceptive products. How would you like a "Solar Powered Clothes Drying System" for just $19.95? Sounds good, right? Until you send off your money and receive a simple 99¢ clothesline. Or, the ad that touted a "secret" system for $10 where you could instantly "double your income." The "system" was a 3x5 card that simply said, "Go to college, studies show that college graduates can earn twice as much per year than non graduates.

Of course these are examples of extreme deception, but ANY sense of deception from your customer will kill any future sales. So concentrate on giving your customers products with a high perceived value. You'll make them happy and maximize your profits at the same time!

BEAT YOUR COMPETITION WITH A GOOD "UMP"!

No, I'm not talking about baseball. I'm referring to the game of business. If you want to succeed, you need a good UMP–a *Unique Marketing Position*. Some refer to it as a Unique Selling Position or something similar. What it means is that you need something that sets you apart from the competition, and makes your product or service more appealing to your specific target market. It is even more important in direct marketing because your customer cannot physically see your product and you do not interact with them face-to-face.

UNDERSTANDING THE IMPORTANCE OF "PPS"...

No, not the PPS in a letter. There are three ways that you can establish a Unique Marketing Position. The first is with the PRODUCT. The second is PRICE. The third is SERVICE. Any one of these alone, or a combination of the three, can be used to create your own Unique Marketing Position. Let's take a closer look at how these are used to set you apart from the rest and make it attractive for customers to purchase from you. Understand that before you create a Unique Marketing Position, you must first define your target market. Without a defined target market that has an unfulfilled need which your product or service will satisfy, the greatest UMP in the world is not going to make one bit of difference.

PRODUCT–Simply put, if you have a product that nobody else is selling, you are unique and customers are going to purchase from you. This of course assumes that the product is in demand by your target market. This does NOT mean that you have to invent some new product. It means that you should be the only source, or one of a handful of sources, from whom your customer can purchase this product. For example, if you import a product and secure exclusive U.S. distribution rights, you have an advantage over anybody else trying to sell the same product. Remember though that very few products are so unique that they cannot be duplicated.

Another way to set yourself apart from your competition is to market a product of superior quality. I know that I purchase many items by mail order because of the quality. Retail stores, especially "Discount Stores", are more likely to carry products that are the most popular, not necessarily the best quality. If you offer a product with a quality that cannot be readily obtained at the retail level, you can have a lot of success in selling that product.

Still another way to differentiate yourself with a product is by offering a larger selection than your competition. Remember, in mail order you are not only competing against other mail order companies, you are also competing against retail outlets. However, retail outlets don't always have a complete selection of product. In mail order you can offer a HUGE product selection without having to carry a lot of inventory. How? By using drop shipping. By arranging to have your product drop shipped by the factory or distributor you can offer a much larger selection that most retail outlets.

PRICE–Obviously, if you can offer the same product as others at a lower price you are going to have an advantage. This is especially important if your product is not unique. For example, if you are selling name brand stereo equipment at a much lower price than other sellers, you have a Unique Marketing Position. This is because the customer can easily reference the price of the product from many different sellers since it is the same item from every source. In mail order, you can often sell a product more cheaply because of the reduced overhead as compared to retail operations. For example, I recently purchased a new softball bat from a small mail order company. This bat sells for $300 at every sporting goods store around. This little mail order company sells the exact same bat for $235. So, I saved $65 and did not have to pay sales tax to boot!

Don't be so quick to lower your price, unless you are using that as your Unique Marketing Position. A lower price might generate more sales, but may not necessarily translate into more profits.

SERVICE–This is one that is so often overlooked, but can be the most important Unique Marketing Position of all. Think of the stores you frequent. If you're like me, many times you'll pay a little more for a product because you like the store and the customer service you receive. Convenience is also included in "Service" as it relates to establishing a Unique Marketing Position…. Just like the local 7-11 that charges up to 30% or more for the same product you can buy at the grocery store. The fact that they offer convenience outweighs the higher price.

While customer service should always be a top priority, it is especially important in mail order. You MUST have repeat sales to succeed. One way to ensure repeat sales is by making your customers feel appreciated. Make sure that everyone in your organization treats customers with respect, and be willing to give a little extra. It will pay off down the road with repeat sales. Of course, this does NOT mean you have to put up with abusive or non-profitable customers. Let's face it, some customers are more trouble than they're worth and are looking for something for nothing. The more you give them, the more they want and the less they appreciate it. Don't waste your time with these types of customers.

IF YOU WANT TO BURY YOUR COMPETITION–GET YOURSELF AN "IMP!"

No, not your own little elf, although that would be kind of neat. I'm referring to an Irreplaceable Marketing Position. This is where you offer a Product, Price or Service so unique that you are "irreplaceable." Maybe it's through a product that you patent, or a service that nobody else provides, or a price so low that your competition cannot touch you. It's difficult, but not impossible, to establish yourself as an irreplaceable source in the minds of your customers. This is the key. Make them THINK that you are irreplaceable. For example, in my import business my customers use me because of the knowledge I have importing products from overseas. While there are many things I share with my customers, I do NOT share everything. I don't share my unique sources, the tricks I use to get cheaper freight or the specific knowledge I have of U.S. Customs and financial transactions with my vendors. If I shared all of this information with my customers, they might think that they do not need me and go directly to my sources. I'd much rather have them think that I am an irreplaceable part of their buying process.

Think of the things that you can do to make yourself irreplaceable. Are you the only one offering the product or service? Can you sell it so much cheaper than anybody else that nobody can compete with you? Can you offer a unique customer service or guarantee? Can you obtain exclusive rights to a product? These ways in which you can make yourself "Irreplaceable."

There's an old saying in business that says to be successful you must be first, better or cheaper. If you can be the first or only one to offer a product or service, offer a better one or a cheaper one you can begin to establish a strong Unique Marketing Position or, better yet, an Irreplaceable Marketing Position. Your success is sure to follow!

HOW TO USE AND CHOOSE EFFECTIVE MAILING LISTS

So, you ordered a list of "opportunity" seekers from one of the cheapie ads in the mail order publications, did your first mailing of 1,000 pieces and anxiously started counting your riches, just waiting for all that money to come pouring in from your latest efforts. You waited, and waited, and–nothing! Oh, maybe a few orders here and there, but not even enough to come close to breaking even. Congratulations, your direct mailing campaign just BOMBED! Why do I say "congratulations"? I am not being sarcastic or cruel. You see, this is where you get to LEARN and correct things so that you can make money in the future. This is where you are either going to find out if you are just looking for a "get-rich-quick" scheme, or if you really want to operate a legitimate business of your own. You must experience failure before you can achieve success. Rarely do people make money on their first direct mail campaign. Heck, I've bombed on many of my direct mailings. However, through years of learning and trial and error, I've learned to minimize my chances of failing.

IT MUST BE THE LIST, RIGHT?

Invariably, the first thing most people do when their direct mailing bombs is claim that they got a lousy list. It's true, the list is extremely important. However, the list must be a good fit to the OFFER you are mailing or you're doomed for failure. For example, if you're selling a book on how to maintain and clean fireplaces you would not only want a list of homeowners, but you'd want to be sure they had fireplaces as well.

The same theory holds true when selling any "how to" information or money making opportunity. It's quite possible that the list you are using is too good for your offer! That's right, it's too good because the list contains names of people that are too knowledgeable for your offer. For example, let's say you purchase a list of "Opportunity Buyers" that have actually paid money for a business opportunity within the last 30 days or so. These people are looking for legitimate opportunities. If you send them some pyramid, bogus MLM or chain letter scheme do you really think you'll be successful? Of course not. These folks have already been bombarded by similar offers and are too smart to buy into such nonsense. You will get a very poor return, but it is not the fault of the list! On the other hand, if you offered these people a workable, realistic opportunity to earn money you might realize a very good return indeed.

WHERE DO YOU FIND THE RIGHT LIST TO MATCH YOUR OFFER?

This is the million-dollar question! If the answer were easy there would be many more successful direct mail companies. First of all, stay away from "Cheap" lists. This is a mistake that many make when purchasing lists. They buy the cheapest lists available, without investigating if they are any good. Look at the big picture here. If you pay $50 more for a list of 1,000 names this is only 5¢ more per name. If you are selling something that nets you a $10 profit, you only need 5 more orders for the more expensive list to pay off. This is only a .005 percent increase in response. A better list can easily net you a 2% or 3% higher response, so it pays to buy the better list. Beware of the "Opportunity Seeker" lists. Many of these are names compiled from generic ads such as *"EARN $1,000 A WEEK NOW! FREE REPORT, CALL 1-800-XXX-XXXX!"* This ad may generate a lot of leads, but they are not "qualified" (willing to spend money for your particular type of offer). These names are worthless.

If you want a list of names to match your particular offer, a good place to start is with a reputable list broker. Brokers work with several different lists and can custom tailor one for you. I'm not talking about someone calling himself or herself a "broker" that just sells one type of list. I'm talking about REAL list brokers here. You'll find them in phone books, trade publications, or in the *Standard Rate and Data* (SRDS) reference directory at your library. They will take a look at your offer and work with you to obtain a list of buyers interested in what you are selling. The more detailed you get, the more expensive the list. You will also be required to purchase a minimum of 5,000 names. The SRDS reference book is an invaluable tool when searching for lists to match your offer. It lists thousands of lists, list brokers and other sources with all the pertinent details (cost per thousand, age, compiled or response, etc.) you'll need to make an informed decision about who to contact.

The BEST place to purchase names is directly from a prime source. This is somebody that is actually compiling "qualified" leads for their own offers, which compliment what you are selling. For example, if you are selling a book on how to lose weight, you may rent a list from a company selling diet related nutritional products. These are complimentary products. If the prime source has a large enough database, they may have an outside list management company handling their list rentals. The most important thing for you to do is find out as much as you can about the names. Ask how they are compiled, how much they spent on average, how old they are, how many times they have been rented, etc.

The absolute best list you can use is your own "In-House" list! These are the names you acquire from people answering your ads and ordering your products. For people that actually order, you should mail to these names over and over again–always trying to sell them something else and, preferably, getting them to buy higher and higher priced products.

As for the inquiry names, you should mail to these people more than once as well. Mail to them at least three times and maybe even more. The point is, mail to them until you are not seeing a positive result from your mailings.

You can also make another income from "renting" your lists–both your buyers and your inquiry names. People in the business who sell products similar to yours will pay good money for these names, as will mailing list companies. As you grow and establish a list of a few thousand or so names, you can contact other companies to see if they wish to purchase, or rent, the names you have. There are also companies that will purchase your inquiry envelopes. The going rate is anywhere from 10¢ to 25¢ per name. You won't have to worry about contacting most of these companies, they'll contact you as you place more and more ads. This is just an additional stream of income for you. Just be sure that, before you sell your inquiry envelopes or names, you log the names into your own data files so that you can use them.

WHAT ABOUT YOUR OFFER?

Quite honestly, most of the offers I see are garbage. Do you really think that people are going to believe you're making a fortune when you send out some flyer that looks like it was photocopied at the local drug store? Or maybe you've got a professionally printed sales package but you're promoting an illegal pyramid or chain. People are getting hit with these offers everyday and it doesn't take long before they discount all of them as garbage. The most important thing to remember here is that you MUST have a product or service that people want or need. In other words, it answers an unfulfilled want or desire. The market must also be large enough that there are enough people that will order your product or service. The price must be such that you will make a profit from a reasonable return. I always shoot to break even on a 1% return. If I can't do that, I don't bother with the campaign.

Test, Test and Test Again!

Hmm, seems like this is a recurring topic in the book, eh? You bet it is. Because TESTING is the most important strategy in marketing and advertising! I'll refer to it again and again, for good reason. Before you go blowing a bunch of money on any offer or list do a reasonable test. Since there are SO MANY variables involved in any direct mail campaign, you must first test the list. Mail out to about 10% of the names and gauge the response. If it is not favorable, do NOT mail to the rest of the names. Try changing your offer slightly (maybe a different sales letter, circular, etc) and test again. Test ONE variable at a time so you know what it is that works.

Direct mail can be a long, tedious process. You must offer a product that is desired and has enough margin to sell via direct mail. It is a learning process, like anything else that is worthwhile. Don't try to take steps that are too big. Take little steps, adjusting and tweaking your offer and strategy each step of the way until you find something that works.

PREMIUMS VS. DISCOUNTS WHICH ARE BETTER?

You want your prospects to buy what you're selling–right now! You've got to get people to act. In order to do that you must give them a little extra incentive. You know, make them think that if they don't act now they will miss out on something that will truly benefit them. Two common methods used to give the potential buyer a reason to buy right away are the use of discounts and premiums.

Just what are discounts and premiums, and why are they so essential to direct marketing? A discount is a reduction off the normal selling price of an item. Usually, you offer a discount in conjunction with a deadline for the purchase. For example, "purchase this product within the next ten days and receive $10.00 off the purchase price". The discount is given as either a dollar figure or a percentage off.

Premiums, on the other hand, are merchandise offered at a low cost or free as an incentive to purchase a particular product or service. For example, *"purchase this product within the next ten days and receive a free book valued at $19.95"*. There are other incentives you can use to entice people to buy, such as rebates, contests, sweepstakes, coupons, etc. However, these are usually not effective for direct marketing so I won't deal with them here.

It is essential to use some sort of offer over and above the basic product or service you are selling in order to get people to act. Which is better? In almost all cases in direct marketing (or mail order, direct mail, it's all the same thing) it's much better to offer a premium as opposed to a discount. In my experience, a well thought out premium, with a high "perceived" value will outperform a discount offer by a margin of two to one. Why? For several reasons. First, let's take a look at when you should use a discount.

Discounts are very effective when you are selling a consumer product that has an easily identifiable price point. For example, if you're selling a well-known brand of stereo you may offer a discount of $50 off your normal retail price. This is effective if: 1) The product is well known, so the customer knows it's value, and, 2) If your normal retail price is not inflated to begin with. In other words, let's say you offer the stereo at a "discounted price" of $150, claiming a $50 discount. If the potential customer knows that the same brand stereo sells everyday in other catalogs or retail stores for $150, your $50 discount doesn't mean a thing. In fact, your strategy may backfire because the customer may think that you are over-inflating all your prices.

The fact is, when you offer a discount people don't necessarily see the true value. He or she thinks the product is only worth what you're selling it for with the discount. So, the discount offer loses its effectiveness. Also, when you give a discount, it's cash off your bottom line! You are losing $50 worth of profit on that stereo! So, how do we get around these problems and still entice the customer? By offering a PREMIUM.

Premiums are very effective at getting customers to buy. Better yet, they actually cost you less money than discounts. Using our example with the stereo, let's say you offer FREE speakers, valued at $50, with the purchase. Now you've got an incentive! The customer knows the speakers are worth $50 because that's what you sell them for everyday, and your price is not inflated. However, in **ACTUALITY,** these speakers might only cost you $20 to purchase. So now you get the full price for the stereo, and give away the speakers. Your actual cost for the premium is $20, but the customer gets a $50 "perceived" value. See how effective this can be? It's a win-win situation for you and your customers. The higher the perceived value of the premium, and the lower your actual cost, the better off you will be. Be sure the premium is something that the potential customer will want!

In direct mail, where much of the product sold is information, premiums are especially effective. If you sell a book for $20, the customer knows the value is twenty bucks. Now, if you offer a FREE book, also worth $20, if he or she purchases within ten days the customer "perceives" the value of the premium to be $20. Your actual cost to print the book might be two dollars. So, it costs you two bucks to make the customer think they are getting a $20 value, which they are.

You should **ALWAYS** offer a premium when selling information via direct mail. The premium should be tied in with a dated offer. In other words *"order within ten days and receive..."* It increases your response rate, gives the customer a reason to order right away, and makes your customer feel like you are giving them something for nothing. Believe it or not, people like to feel that they are receiving something for nothing. It is much more effective than simply offering them a cash discount.

Many times people will order from you for the premium, and not necessarily for what you are selling! Think of Sports Illustrated. They offer a FREE video for new subscribers, or a basketball, or something similar. Many people order the subscription just to get the premium. Did Sports Illustrated lose money? Not really. First of all, the premium actually costs them a fraction of its perceived "value". Secondly, they now have you as a subscriber and hope that you renew year after year. However, they only give you the premium once! This is a strategic direct marketing technique.

Think about your own offers. Certainly there is something you can offer as a premium–perhaps a report or booklet. The trick is to offer as high a "perceived" value premium as you can, without high cost to you. This is why printed premiums are so powerful. Test different premiums and offers. When you hit on a good one, you'll see a dramatic increase in your sales!

ADVERTISING YOUR PRODUCTS

If you remember nothing else from this book or anything else you read about mail order, remember this: It's not what you sell, it's HOW you sell it! Please read that statement again and again. It's not necessarily the PRODUCT that's important, it's HOW you advertise the product which makes people respond.

DISPLAY ADVERTISING

Display ads, also referred to as print or space ads, are advertisements that appear in printed magazines, papers, tabloids and other publications. These ads are excellent for promoting mailing lists. However, it is difficult to sell anything directly from a display ad smaller than $^1/_4$ page. In other words, you just want to get a prospect to answer your ad. At that point you send them a complete sales package, including the mailing list circular. If you want to run larger size ads asking for orders, called "direct response ads" you can do so, but don't try it until you have established your business and can afford it. Large display ads are expensive to run.

Advertising can be expensive, especially in the higher circulation opportunity publications, so you want to start slow. There are many smaller circulation publications that target the business and money-making opportunity market, as well as nearly every other market you may be interested in selling your products to. You can place a 2" ad for as little as $15 or so. This is a great way to test your ads.

Most prime sources will provide you with camera-ready ads. You can use these when you first start, but I would suggest taking the time to learn how to write your own ads. You can then either typeset them yourself or have them done. With the desktop publishing programs available today and a little bit of computer knowledge, you can easily become a typesetting whiz in no time. Microsoft Publisher™ is an excellent software program to use for designing your own ads and marketing materials.

CLASSIFIED ADVERTISING

Placing small classified ads is an inexpensive, effective strategy for generating prospects for your mail order product or service. Do NOT ever, ever, ever try to sell anything directly from a classified ad (except personal items of course). There is just not enough room to explain what you are selling and ask for money. Besides, that is not the purpose of a classified, especially when it comes to selling mailing lists. All you want to do is generate prospects or leads so that you can then send them your sales information. A small classified ad might cost just $80 or so in a fairly large circulation publication and much less in smaller publications. However, this $80 is a small investment if it generates quality prospects. The key is to convert these prospects into sales!

When placing classifieds, you want to find publications that are already offering products similar to yours. Do not worry about seeing other companies offering products like yours, this is what you want. Especially check past issues to see if they have been running for a while. This tells you that the ads are probably working or else they would not continue running. It also tells you that your product will interest the readers of that particular publication, i.e., you are reaching your "target market." You are hopefully going to be offering a much better product with powerful sales materials of your own. Stay away from publications that do not offer products similar to yours in their advertising sections. Don't think that success lies in new territories in this case. You'll only waste your money. You do not need to reinvent the wheel here, place your ads where others have already had success.

USING AN 800# WITH YOUR CLASSIFIEDS

There is another method of using classified advertising, which is very effective. This is to place a classified ad, but have an 800-voicemail box set up where the person responding to the ad can call. It is here that you give them a 3-minute or so sales message to really try and close the deal and get them to send off for more information. You just ask them to leave their name and address, and then you mail information to them. This method works well from a cost per inquiry standpoint. For the small cost of a classified, plus about $20 a month to rent the 800 number mailbox, you can generate a lot of quality leads. You can use your message to really reinforce the benefits of your product. You can also further qualify your prospects depending on what you say in your message. There are many companies that offer 800 number mailbox services. The one I've used for years is **DigitCom Services, Inc**. You can call them at (800) 545-1466 or write them at 12923 Venice Blvd., Los Angeles, CA 90066. Tell them TJT Marketing Associates, #1387, referred you.

Whenever you place display or classified ads be sure and code your ads. This is so that you can tell which publication the response or order came from. Coding ads is easy. You may use a department or suite number in your address, which you designate for each publication. Or, you can simply use a code in your address. For example, "Box 123-A", where the "A" is the code for the publication containing your ad. For direct mail pieces, you can simply ad a code number on the order form.

I've included a resource guide with this kit. It contains a list of several publications targeting the business and moneymaking opportunity market. You should write each of these publications and request a "media kit". Make sure you write a typewritten or computer-generated letter on professional looking letterhead. **No handwritten letters–ever**! Tell them you are interested in possibly placing an ad in their publication. They will send you a rate card, data on their publication and a sample issue. Some of the smaller ones do not have complete media kits, but they will send you a sample issue and rate data.

WRITING ATTENTION GRABBING ADS

All of us in mail order realize the importance of advertising. It is our lifeblood, without it we cannot sell anything. In order for us to effectively market our products or services, we first MUST get our message out. We use advertisements to accomplish this task. But, out of all the ads that appear every day in hundreds of magazines, newspapers, ad sheets, etc., only a handful gets noticed. If your ad does not get noticed, it is worthless. So, it is of utmost importance to use ads that grab attention, hold that attention, and induce the reader to respond!

The first thing to do when you sit down to write an ad, is ask yourself "What am I offering to someone that is a potential customer?" If you cannot answer that question, you are not ready to write an ad. Many ads never answer this question, and they are useless. When writing ads, you must get the reader to feel that you are offering them something that will benefit them in some way. Understand what the key benefit of your product is. People respond and buy based on benefits, not on features. What is the difference? Benefits are things that can help improve the life of the potential customer. Features are just things that the product does. They really do not benefit your customer.

For example, a company I own once sold a personal alcohol tester. The main feature is that it can test the blood alcohol concentration. But, a benefit is that it can save your life, by indicating that you should not drive! So, understand what you are offering, and write all the BENEFITS down in order of importance. Then, you can structure your ad to communicate those benefits.

Now, once you clearly define the benefits of your product, it is time to write your ad. There are five fundamentals of writing a good advertisement. A powerful ad will include all five, in order. They are:

1. **Grab the readers attention**

2. **Show the advantage of your product**

3. **Prove the advantage with facts**

4. **Show people they need the advantage**

5. **Ask for action**

Grab attention with a powerful HEADLINE! The headline is the most important part of the ad. If the headline does not grab attention, the rest of the ad is useless because it will not be read. Think of how you read a newspaper, or classified section. You scan the pages and stop at the headlines that grab your attention. This is what you want to do with *your* headline. You want to make the reader STOP and read your ad! The headline must get immediate attention. The headline should be relatively short, contain powerful wording, mention the benefit, and make the selling promise, all very quickly and clearly.

The headline should appeal on emotion. People react to emotional words and phrases. The headline should also be freestanding. In other words it could make sense without the rest of the copy. This is where clarity comes into play. For example, your headline could read, "Make One Million Dollars-Guaranteed". This is certainly attention grabbing, but is not clear. It is too vague. If you say, "Make One Million Dollars Selling Books By Mail Order" the headline is much clearer, and will induce more people to read your ad.

Use powerful words that evoke emotion and attract attention. Some examples are free, Rich, Secret, Amazing, Bargain, Learn, Earn, Proven, Safe, No Risk, Increase, etc. Use these words, but do not overuse them! Too many of these words will dilute the effectiveness of your headline.

Once you grab the reader's interest, you must get them to read the ad, and KEEP their interest. This is where you show people how, and why your product will be useful to them. You must answer: "What will your product do for me?" Do not show what the product is, show what it can do! Sell the "sizzle, not the steak". Appeal to the emotions, for they are the primary motivating factors for action.

Next, you must prove your claims. Back it up with actual facts and numbers, not just statements. Do not say, "Increase your income", but

"Increased John Doe's income by 50% in six months". There is a greater impact by stating facts.

Once you have proven your claims, you must persuade the customer to act. This is where you sum up all the benefits, and the emotional motivators. You are bringing it all together here, and then you are going to ask for-ACTION!

Now, you must ask the reader to act on your ad. Do not assume anything here. People need to be induced to action. This is where you tell them how to order, where to send for more information, whatever the purpose of your ad was. Use inducements like a free offer, a time limit, a limited supply, or some other reason to act right away. Use active language, like "hurry", "act now", "call today", or similar phrases. The point is to get the reader to stop what they are doing and act on your ad!

A powerful, attention-grabbing ad can sell a mediocre product. On the other hand, the best product in the world will fail if it is not advertised right! Take your time, and write your ad several different ways. Ask people to read different renditions, and pick the one that evokes the best response. Then, test the ad! Test several different ads for the same product. Test the ads in low cost publications, and monitor the results. Once you find one version that is outputting all the others, use that ad in bigger publications. But, TEST the ads first! Sometimes, just changing the headline, or even a word or two in the headline will have dramatic results on the pulling power of an ad!

Remember one other thing when preparing ads. Know your purpose! In other words, is the ad designed to get people to send in money, or is it designed to get qualified leads only. The latter is what is referred to as a two-step ad, where people send for more information and you then send them additional sales materials. Classified or small display ads are usually two-step ads.

Never use classified or small display ads to ask for money, unless the product costs under $10.00. There is simply not enough space to fully convey your product's benefits and to persuade people to send money.

So many mail-order beginners make the mistake of asking for money in classified or small display ads-*Do not do it!* If your product is under $10.00 you may. But, quite frankly, if you want to make real money in mail order you should not be selling products for under $10.00.

When writing two-step ads, remember that you want "good prospects", not just curiosity seekers. So, be careful not to make your ads too general. For example, a classified ad that reads "Secret way to make $ 5,000 per month-send for FREE Details" will generate a lot of responses. But, will they be interested in what you are selling? The ad is not clear enough with regard to exactly what it is you are selling. So, you will have curiosity seekers, but not necessarily good prospects. In this case, the cost of sending sales materials to too many curiosity seekers may outweigh the benefits of the ad.

In summary, you should adhere to the five fundamentals in order to write powerful ads. Be sure to use powerful headlines, and be clear as to exactly what it is you are selling. Do not try to trick or deceive people, they will not like it, and will not respond to your ads.

Writing ads is a special skill, which can be learned. There are many, many books and courses available on the subject of ad writing. Visit your library or bookstore and you'll be amazed at the information you can gather. If you want to learn how to write great ads, I highly suggest the following books:

- "How To Write A Good Advertisement"–Victor O. Schwab

- "Tested Advertising Methods"–John Caples

- "Direct Mail Copy That Sells"–Herschell Gordon Lewis

- "Money In Your Mailbox"–L. Perry Wilbur

DESIGN YOUR ADS TO PULL ORDERS!

One day I received a letter from an advertiser, asking me why his ad was not pulling. He stated that he was running the ad in several different publications, with little response. He wanted to place the ad with me to "*see if your newsletter goes out to more responsive people*" (at that time I accepted ads in the newsletter, a practice I stopped in 1999 because I got tired of all the garbage being advertised and thought it a disservice to my subscribers). I took one look at the ad and sent it back to him. The reason? I knew that the ad was not going to pull in my publication, or any other publication for that matter. Oh the ad was nicely designed, had a neat border and a catch phrase in the headline. It was clear and concise. However, there were two things that shouted out "*LOSER*" upon a first glance. First of all, the ad talked about a product, but never indicated a benefit for the buyer. Secondly, it never asked for action! These are two common mistakes that novices, and even some so-called "experts," make when designing and writing ads. So, let's take a look at how you design an ad that will generate response!

It is a well-known fact that the headline is the most important feature of any ad. If the headline does not grab a prospect's attention the rest of the ad is worthless. Be careful not to be too cute with your headline. Many times I see ads where the headline is some sort of play on words, or a joke of some type. This is a powerful tactic but **ONLY** if the audience knows what you are talking about! Just because you think a headline is catchy does not mean everyone will "*get the point*". So, be careful when trying to be cute or funny. It can backfire.

Most importantly, the headline should convey the most important benefit to the potential customer. Of course, this assumes that you know who your potential customer is! If you do not know who your target customer is, you have no business writing an ad. So be sure you have done your homework and know EXACTLY to whom you are trying to sell!

List all of the benefits of your product or service. This is where many ad writers take the wrong track. *Do not confuse benefits with product features!* For example, if you were selling an orthopedic chair you would NOT emphasize the quality construction, materials, color, etc. These are all FEATURES and, while important, they will NOT make someone purchase the chair. Instead, emphasize the fact that it will eliminate backaches, allow for comfortable sitting, help improve posture, etc. These are all BENEFITS. Always look at your product or service from the CUSTOMER'S point of view, not yours. The customer wants to know *"what's in it for me?"* They need to know WHY they should purchase your product. Will it help them do things faster or better? Improve their physical or mental well-being? Allow them to be more socially acceptable? Make them richer? You get the point. You have to answer HOW your product or service will somehow enrich their life! Look at the ads for cars, food, cosmetics, electronics-everything! The most successful advertising campaigns drill into the consumer's head the **BENEFITS** that they achieve from purchasing the product. They appeal to emotional aspects such as fear, wealth, vanity, popularity and similar themes.

So take your product and list all the benefits. Don't think at first, just start listing the benefits as they pop into your head, one after the other. Now set the list aside and forget it for a day or two. Then, go back and look at it. Add to it if you can and then really study your list. Start arranging the benefits in the order of importance. Don't be subjective here, get other people's opinions. If feasible, get the opinions of potential customer's from your chosen target market. Once you have the most important benefit clearly defined, design a headline around **THAT** benefit! Throw in a few attention grabbing words or phrases such as FREE, NEW, INCREDIBLE, AMAZING, LIMITED and ACT NOW! Don't go overboard with them, too many will make your ad seem amateurish and less believable.

Once the headline is complete start with the body of the ad. Incorporate all of the important benefits from your list into action generating copy, always thinking to yourself *"what is in it for my customer"*. Use clear, concise language and get to the point quickly. Keep the copy moving so that the reader stays focused and interested. If your ad has room for a graphic by all means use one. However, don't just indiscriminately throw graphics in an ad. Make sure that they make sense, are clear, and relate to your product or service. It is OK to be funny, if that is the theme to your ad. But remember what I said before and be SURE that your target market will understand the humor!

Finally, ask for action. This is a part many people forget. You have to make your customer want to call or write for an order or more information, *NOW!* Make it easy with an 800 number, credit card acceptance, special bonuses, anything that will make them act quickly and with as little effort as possible! Put a time limit on the offer or offer a special incentive for ordering early. If the item is costly offer installment payments-"*3 easy payments of $19.95*" sounds better than *$59.95.* You have the customer's attention, they have read your ad all the way to the end. Don't lose them now-*get them to act!*

I cannot stress enough the importance of consumer oriented advertising as opposed to institutional type advertising. Institutional ads tell about the product's features. They are targeted to people in the industry that are going to purchase the product for resale. Even these ads stress benefits, but not so much the consumer benefits. Consumer ads stress benefits to the final purchaser-the target customer.

I recall a few years back, I developed an ad campaign for a new line of high-tech automotive gauges. I thought I had the greatest ad campaign ever-really stressing the technological advancements and coming up with a great catch phrase. I discussed the ads with several colleagues and industry experts and they all agreed that they were a sure winner.

We placed the ads in consumer-oriented publications and *the campaign bombed!* That was many years ago and I learned an important lesson. I realized that first of all I did not look at the product from a consumer's point of view, but rather from a seller's. I spent a lot of time stressing product features and advancements, but ignored the BENEFITS to the consumer! These gauges were easy to install, easier to read making them safer, upgraded the car's interior to look high tech. And, hey they just looked "cool". These were all BENEFITS I ignored. All was not lost though, I used the ad campaign at the trade level as institutional ads and they were a winner! But as consumer ads, they stunk!

Writing great ads takes time and patience. Always remember to look at it from your customer's vantage point and you have half the battle won!

TRACKING YOUR ADS

In addition to coding and testing your ads, you need to track them as well. Make yourself a form that shows the name of the ad, where it was placed, the number of inquiries and the total sales. Your form may look something like this:

Advertisement: Weight Loss Book		Publication/Issue: Health Magazine/Jan., 02		Code: XZ	
Cost: $210.00		Orders To Breakeven:		18	
Date	Inquiries	Inquires To Date	Sales	Sales To Date	
01/15/02	3	7	2	4	
01/17/02	4	11	3	7	

The above is just a one example of the type of form you can use. It really doesn't matter WHAT form you use as long as YOU can track the ad and see if it is working or not. I always like to put the "Break Even" number right on the form. This way I can tell at a glance how many sales I need for the ad to pay for itself. For example, let's say the above ad cost $210 and the book sells for $25. You might think if you sell 9 books the ad paid for itself, not so. You need to figure the actual PROFIT you make. So, lets say after shipping, the actual cost, etc. the book costs you $13 to acquire (or produce) and ship. So, your actual PROFIT on each sale is $12. You would need 18 sales to break even.

If you are not selling the product directly from the ad and are using the ad to generate inquiries only, you still need to track the ad. Make sure it is pulling well, and that enough of the inquirers are actually buying the product to make the ad worthwhile. However, advertising is not ALWAYS about direct sales...

HOW TO MAKE ADVERTISING PAY, EVEN WHEN THERE ARE NO SALES

Several years ago I was working on an advertising campaign and lamenting over the poor response. One of my mentors at the time asked me what the problem was. I replied that the ad failed to pay for itself. He asked me "are you planning on being in business for awhile?" "Well, yes," I replied. He then asked, "Are you going to develop and sell other products?" I answered that I was and he said, "then your advertising did not fail. The point of true advertising is NOT to sell product, but to make your market aware of who you are and what you do." That's when it hit me, I was concentrating too much on the actual sales generated from the ads and less on the big picture and the long range results from a continued advertising effort.

Unfortunately, most people who start mail order companies fail to realize that advertising is not strictly about sales. It's more about building a company, product or brand awareness within your specified target market. Even if an ad does not pay for itself in sales, it can still be an effective promotional tool for your business. Too often people get caught up in the actual sales of an ad instead of the effect it has on generating responses or inquiries. Or, at the very least, putting your name in front of the customer again and again.

I was reminded of this fact the other day while watching a basketball game on TV as I was working out. If you've ever seen an NBA or college game on the tube lately, you'll notice an ever-changing banner of ads right under the scorer's table, directly in line with the cameras. These banners advertise all kinds of things. Suddenly, an ad for Dunkin' Donuts popped up. Right in the middle of doing some arm curls I saw this and suddenly had a taste for a Dunkin' Donut's chocolate donut. It brought back memories of special Sunday mornings after church when the old man would treat us to some donuts. Believe me, it was rare.

Did that ad try to sell me a particular donut? No. Did it even mention a Dunkin' Donut's location? Nope. All it did was put that name out there and my emotions did the rest. For three days I had that craving until I finally couldn't take it anymore and traveled 15 miles to the nearest Dunkin' Donuts to satisfy my craving. So now I had to work out twice as hard that particular night, but that's another story.

This is the true power of advertising—repetitive bombardments to your target market, advertising your products and/or services. Of course if you are placing an ad directly selling a product, what we call a direct response ad, you want it to pay off. However, this is not the only reason for advertising. I have many ads that don't sell a thing—they just ask to call us or write us for information. I also continue to run ads that don't pay off on the front-end. However, the responses I receive often turn into back-end sales, which make the ad worthwhile.

Most importantly, it's the fact that our ads run—again and again—and people start to recognize our name, logo, and products, whatever it may be. I get calls all the time from people who say "I've seen your ads running for a long time and I decided to give you a try," or something to that effect. So it was not ONE single ad that got the business, it was a continuous effort and series of ads.

Don't make the worst mistake of all when starting an ad campaign—trying to sell something from a small display or classified ad. Instead, you want a REACTION to the ad—be it a phone call, reply by mail, a visit to your Web Site or some other action. You can ask for a couple of bucks if you want, but make sure your ad is compelling enough for people to cough up the couple of bucks AND be sure to give them something worthwhile. However, if you are betting your business survival on making money from a small ad asking for a couple of bucks forget it. What you want are PROSPECTS and, more importantly, you want those prospects to respond—either to your current ad or to one at a later date because they "recognized" your company name.

You can also use "loss leaders" to draw people to your company. Just like retail stores, you can actually lose money on a popular seller just to get customers to give you a try. You can then promote your other products and make money on the back-end sales.

If you are in mail order, or any business, you have got to advertise. There is no way around it. However, if you don't have continuous advertising campaigns you are not going to succeed. I see many people who place one ad and when it doesn't work they don't place another, or they wait two or three months and then place another ad. You've got to do it ALL the time. Set up an advertising budget and use that budget every month to continue to place ads. If an ad is not successful, change it a bit and continue testing, but don't stop advertising.

With all your ads, make the objective to let people know who you are and what you sell. If you are selling one product now that a potential customer is not interested in buying, that's OK. Perhaps the next product you advertise WILL interest him or her and they will order because your name has been in front of them several times in the past.

This same theory holds true in direct mailing as well. It is sometimes necessary to hit the same list two, three or more times in order to maximize your response. I know from our own postcard mailings that our response is about the same for the first three mailings. Usually on the fourth mailing we see a drop off in response, percentage wise. However, the first three mailings all made money, many times because people recognize the name and it triggers something to make them respond the second or third time they see it.

Advertising does not have to generate sales. It should generate potential sales. Once you get the prospects it is up to YOU to close the deal and sell them on your product or service. Just like your favorite restaurant, you may go there the first time because of an ad you saw or a special promotion. However, you keep going back because you like the food and service. Mail order is no different, but first you have to make yourself known. This should be the focus of your ad campaigns.

COMMON AD WRITING MISTAKES THAT WILL KILL YOUR RESPONSE RATE–AND HOW TO AVOID THEM

You read and hear all kinds of advice from Direct Marketers, yours truly included, on how to write response-generating ads. You know that you need to follow the AIDA formula: Get *Attention*, create *Interest*, generate a *Desire* and ask for *Action*. It goes without saying that every successful ad adheres to this tried and true formula. However, there are a few things you should NOT do when writing ads. You don't read too much about what *NOT* to do, until now that is. I am going to discuss with you some common ad writing mistakes that kill response rates.

UNFOCUSED HEADLINES

The headline is the most important component of your ad. If people don't stop to read your headline, they're not going to read your ad. However, many times headlines are not focused. They do not tell your prospect how the product you are going to sell is going to benefit him or her. DO NOT fall into the trap of using headlines that focus on more than one benefit. Multi-benefit headlines may draw attention, but they are hard to support in the rest of the ad because your focus is not clearly defined. When writing an ad, focus on the GREATEST BENEFIT your product offers and write your headline to support that benefit. For example, if your headline says: "LOSE WEIGHT! GET FIT!" you have a dual benefit. Which are you trying to sell? The weight loss or the fitness aspect? While the two certainly go together, the impact of the headline is diminished. The better thing to do is use sub-headings to support or compliment your main headline.

Another mistake with headlines is not supporting the headline with the rest of the copy. If your headline says "Earn $1,000 A Week", the rest of your ad copy had better tell the reader how they are going to earn $1,000 a week, or create a benefit-rich picture of how their life will improve by earning $1,000 a week. Many times you'll see ads for MLM programs with a headline promising great earnings and then the ad copy stresses the company–long history, good record, great products, etc. So what? What in the world does that have to do with telling you how to earn money? The copy does not support the headline. When I write ad copy, I first come up with a headline, and this might take me an entire day! Don't write just one headline, or even ten. Write several and then narrow them down until you get the one that you like best. Once I have my headline, I write the copy. Anything in the copy that does not support or substantiate my headline is eliminated. If your headline is strong, and your copy tells the prospect how your product or service will give him or her that benefit in your headline, you're on your way to a great ad. The rest is just fluff, and fluff doesn't sell!

CLAIMS THAT CANNOT BE QUANTIFIED

Many times ads have exaggerated claims that cannot be measured against some benchmark. For example, I saw an ad the other day for a sports related product that said you could gain a "1500% edge over your competition." First of all, 1500% is clearly an exaggerated number. Secondly, 1500% of what? This is an empty claim, which cannot be quantified. Now, if the copy said "studies show athlete's using our system increase their 40-yard dash speed by 40%!"-Now you have a quantified statement that can be measured and its impact is much more believable and effective. Percentages are like statistics–they only mean something if they can be measured against a known benchmark. Stay away from unbelievable claims and exaggerations. Ads that claim you can make a million dollars are useless. However, ads that show a believable number, like $750 a week, are much more likely to draw a response.

THE CLASSIC OVERSELL AND FORGETTING TO ASK FOR THE ORDER

I remember when I first started my business career, fresh out of college, I went on a sales call with my boss. I gave a presentation to our prospect and thought I was quite impressive. When we left, I was feeling pretty good until my boss asked me how I thought it went. "It went great", I said, "I think the buyer was really impressed". My boss looked at me and asked, "Where is the order?" Then it hit me-I'd made a classic sales mistake. Actually, I'd made two of them. First of all, I oversold my prospect. Secondly, I forgot to ask for the order, figuring it would come later on.

The same mistakes are made in ad writing. Don't write to impress yourself, write to get a response from your prospect. All the 50¢ words in the world are not going to help you with an order. Many times I'll read an ad and be ready to respond, but the ad goes on and on and pretty soon I'm not interested anymore-I've been "oversold". "The more you tell, the more you sell" is true ONLY if your copy continues to create interest and desire. Ad writing is not like writing English Literature. Most successful ad copy writing is written on a 5th grade reading level. The best advice is to write how you talk and keep it crisp and to the point. Don't go on too long. Many ads are written as if the writer is trying to convince you how smart and clever he or she is. This is great if you're selling textbooks, but not if you're writing copy for ads. You want to SELL, not impress.

Another tip is to know when to stop writing, and ask for action. I can't believe how many otherwise impressive ads forget this major point. ASK for the order; TELL the prospect what to do. And don't be weak here either. Create a strong closing, asking for action. I like to repeat the major benefit or headline in the last sentence of the ad and then tell the prospect what to do (send money, a SASE, call, etc.) Don't assume that the prospect knows what to do-tell him!

TRYING TO BE TOO CUTE AND/OR TOO FUNNY

Stay away from cute little cartoons and phrases in your ads. First of all, what you think is cute or funny may be offensive or stupid to your prospect. Secondly, your prospect may not get the joke and will only be confused. When writing longer copy or sales materials it is sometimes beneficial to try and be funny–if the humor is easily recognized as such. However, in smaller ads, where space is limited, it's best to leave the humor out. Some ads try to be funny, and spend $1/_2$ of the copy explaining the joke instead of reinforcing the headline.

Obviously, if your selling something that lends itself to a cartoonish nature it is OK to use a cartoon graphic or phrase. However, most of us are trying to sell something a little more serious and the ads should reflect this. Stay away from the sarcasm too. Like my Mom always use to tell me, "nobody likes a wise guy". This is true in ad copy writing as well. Remember that humor is very subjective and not everyone will share your perception of what is funny or cute.

Writing ads is a tedious process that takes a lot of time, patience and practice. There is no 100% success formula. However, there are some basic ideas that have proven successful over the years. There are also things that are proven to be detrimental. I've given you some of the more common mistakes that, in my opinion, will kill your ads. Keep this advice in mind when writing your next ad!

TEST YOUR ADS FOR MAXIMUM RESULTS

It is common knowledge that mailing lists should be tested before doing a "rollout" to all the names on the list. Well, the same applies to advertisements! Before spending a lot of money on any advertisement, you must first test the ad to see whether or not it will succeed. Many mail order dealers get caught up with an ad that they created, and spend a lot of money placing that ad only to find out it simply does not pull. The secret of a successful ad campaign is having a well-written ad, to a targeted market, for a product that they want! All three of these factors must be in place for any direct marketing program to be successful.

Once you have your product and target market established, you are ready to test your ads. First of all, you want to determine if you have a product that will sell. Select a few publications that are circulated to your target market. Start with smaller publications, which have less expensive advertising rates. The purpose is to test the ads, not to do a full-blown campaign! Advertise in no more than six of these publications with the same ad. Be sure to "key" or "code" your ad in such a way that you will know where your responses are coming from. Gauge the responses to these ads to see if there is interest in your product. If you receive no response, you either have a problem with your ad, a problem with the product you are offering, or a possible problem with where you placed the ad. So, you need to change one of the three variables until you are getting a positive response.

Once you are getting a response, it is time to some serious testing. Now start to test one ad against another for the same product. Sometimes just a slight change in the headline can cause a dramatic increase in the response rate. When comparing ads against one another, do not just look at cost per circulation. More important is the response rate for the dollar! Suppose an ad cost you $20, and you get five responses. Each response costs $4. Another ad for the same product costs $40, but brings 20 responses. In this case, each response costs just $2! So, while the ad may cost more, the response per dollar is higher, meaning higher profits! This is the key to testing. Change the ads until you are getting the maximum response per dollar.

Once again, be sure to "key" your ads, and gauge their response. Once you have an ad that works, keep using it in as many publications as you can afford. Be sure the publications target your audience. Keep placing the ads, and gauging the response from different publications. Once you get a good record of the publications that pull the best response rate per dollar, concentrate on those publications and drop the ones that are not working.

The whole point with testing is to be patient. It takes time to test ads and publications. But testing saves money in the long run, and results in greater exposure and response for your advertising dollar. Test headlines, guarantees, price, etc. Take one step at a time and keep fine-tuning your advertising campaigns until you receive results which will make your ads profitable!

DIRECT MARKETING WITH A CONSCIENCE
WALKING THE FINE LINE BETWEEN HYPE AND REALITY

Now some may say that direct marketers have no conscience and in many cases they'd be correct. However, many of us do, in fact, care about what we sell and feel a certain obligation to the people who buy our products and services. In effect, we have a conscience and listen to it often.

First of all, if you are in business you are entitled to make a profit. There is nothing wrong with this. If making a profit is not your primary goal then you will not be in business very long. I wish I could give everything I sell away for free, I really do. However the reality is that I have bills to pay, employees to take care of and vendors to support. If I don't make a profit I'm not going to be able to do this. So don't blame a company for making a profit, it's what makes them able to survive. In my import business I am constantly being hammered on by my customers to lower the price, sometimes to a point where there is no way my suppliers can make any money. I always tell my suppliers to make sure that, whenever they quote me, they have enough of a profit margin to make it worthwhile. If not, it's not going to be a productive relationship because they are not going to make money. Eventually they are going to have to do one of three things: raise their prices, lower the quality or give up the business altogether. None of these is a positive solution.

Unfortunately, many direct marketers, especially those selling "business" or "money-making" opportunities, not only try to make a profit, they do so at the expense of their customers. In other words they rip them off by offering products that are no good or don't come close to living up to the hype they've written about in their marketing materials.

This is a dilemma we direct marketers face all the time. We walk a fine line between hype and response generating advertising. It's just the way it is. The reality is that it DOES take a certain amount of hype in order to generate responses to your advertising. However, we must first determine what we mean by "hype." Hype is defined in the dictionary as "to deceive." Hold on though, it is also defined as "to promote with enthusiasm." See the dilemma? For our purposes, when I refer to hype I am referring to the latter definition. One could also defend hype as "advertising." Like it or not, that's just the way it is.

There are many people out there claiming they are tired of being ripped off and that marketers should be 100% totally honest. This is all well and good, but an awful lot depends on how you define that honesty. Do you really think buying that new car is going to make your life so much better? Or that piece of exercise equipment is automatically going to turn you into a hard body in just a few weeks? Or that a supplement will allow you to eat anything you want and still lose weight? Or that there exists some "program" out there that can earn you a fortune without any work or effort? Of course not, but this is what the ads for these products lead you to believe. The fact that they work is a testament to some powerful advertisements and copywriting. Do some go too far in their claims? Yes. Others don't go far enough. This is the line that exists when marketing products–balancing the hype against the reality while getting people to respond!

When I was in college I had a professor who was a former top-notch copywriter for a leading advertising firm in New York. He'd been responsible for millions and millions of dollars in sales through his ads, all written for clients of the advertising firm. I asked him once why he never started his own business, since he could write copy for almost any product and generate instant sales. He smiled at me and said,

"Because I could never write that much B.S. for a product I was selling myself, it's much easier to hype someone else's product."

There is an old Latin term called "caveat emptor", which means, "Let the buyer beware." Up until the early part of the 20th century this is how business was conducted. This put all the responsibility for sales transactions upon the buyer. As unscrupulous sellers started ripping people off left and right, laws were enacted to protect the buyers. This was good, because it made the seller accountable for what was being sold and cut down on the "snake oil" type of product claims. It also made it tougher for con artists to operate, although it certainly didn't stop them. It did open the door for some pretty creative copywriting and advertising–seeing how far the envelope could be pushed while keeping within the limits of legal advertising. Many unscrupulous sellers ignore the laws anyway, but these are the scam artists. Others write so much hype and untrue product characteristics because they don't know any better and think that this is the way to sell products. They are not scam artists per se; they are just inexperienced copywriters who think if you call a spade something other than a spade it will sell.

As one who does copywriting for both others and myself, I can personally attest to the difficulty of being 100% honest and ethical while at the same time creating sales and advertising pieces that elicit a response. This is not always easy. The reality is that without a certain amount of hype, you will not sell anything. Twenty years ago you could advertise a book about making money in mail order, and call it just that, and it would sell. Today, you must promote it as a "system" or some other secretive product in order for people to respond. This takes some creativity and, yes, a little hype as well.

One thing you should never do is lie. I've said this many times. Don't make claims that are not true. You should also stay away from claims that are overly exaggerated. "Eat Whatever You Want and Lose 20 Pounds In One Week," or "Earn One Million Dollars This Year Working Just 2 Hours A Week" are just not going to cut it. You may get some morons to believe you and order, but more likely you'll end up getting a letter from the FTC for fraudulent advertising.

However, you can certainly use any claims that are personal to you. "I Earn $500 A Week Mailing This Special Letter" is an example of honest hype (providing you DO in fact earn that). Maybe the special "letter" is nothing more than a mailing list flyer. However, if you said THAT you would not get much response.

So, if you want to increase your sales and succeed in direct marketing you are going to have to use hype. Use what I call "good hype," not deceiving or untrue hype. Successful advertisers have been doing this for years and it is the only way you are going to succeed. You should strive to be honest when writing ads and to make sure you feel good about what it is you are selling. More importantly, give people more than they expect when they respond. This will keep your conscious clear.

TO STUFF OR NOT TO STUFF?

That is the question. OK, so it's not as prophetic as "To be or not to be", but we're talking mail order here, not Hamlet. Specifically, we are talking about whether or not to stuff multiple offers in one mailing. There are two schools of thought on this issue. Some think that you should maximize postage and stuff as many offers as you can in one envelope. The thinking is that if someone does not like one of the offers, they may choose one of the other ones. Others think that it is better to concentrate on one offer in an envelope so as not to confuse the potential buyer. The truth is that there are times to stuff and times not to stuff, and knowing the difference can improve your sales dramatically.

Humans have a tendency to think that if a little of something is good, then a lot must be better. We all know that this is not necessarily so. If you have a headache and take a couple aspirin, that is good. However, take the whole bottle and you are going to be in some serious trouble! The same concept is true when dealing with direct mail. A lot is not necessarily better, and in most cases is detrimental to your response rate.

Like anything else in direct marketing, there is never a 100% right way to do something. There are simply too many variables when dealing with mail order to determine what will and will not work for all situations. However, there are some things that are known to decrease response rates, based on years and years of testing. There is a scientific angle to mail order that all successful dealers adhere to. After all, why try to reinvent the wheel when others have already done it? In other words, there are many areas that can be improved. But some are done a certain way for a reason-they work!

So, with that said, let's address the question of "To stuff or not to stuff"? First of all, it has been proven over and over again that you DO NOT increase your chance of making a sale by stuffing a bunch of unrelated offers in one mailing. In fact, the opposite is true. You severely reduce your chance of getting any response because the potential customer is either confused or too busy to look at a bunch of different offers. If you have targeted your market, identified an unfulfilled need, and found a product to fit that need, there is no reason to fill an envelope with a bunch of hoopla! No, you should concentrate on selling your customers ONE item and put together a dynamic sales package which includes a cover letter, brochure or flyer and a reply envelope. How fancy you get depends on your budget and ambition, but these basic essentials should be included. I would much rather put the effort into an excellent sales letter and brochure for one GOOD product then four or five offers for mediocre products. It seems much more professional to a prospective customer, and your credibility is enhanced.

However, many beginners do not yet have that one super product and are feeling their way around and getting their feet wet in mail order. They find it difficult to resist the "more is better" theory and listen to those that believe it is better to stuff more than one offer in an envelope. The truth is, in some instances, this theory is correct. In my experience, if you have inexpensive offers (less than $15.00) or **RELATED** offers (such as typesetting and advertising services) then it is acceptable to include more than one offer in an envelope. However, there are some things that you MUST do if you want to draw responses. First of all, include a cover letter! So many people skip this step and it is essential that you do not! Tell the prospective buyer what the heck it is that you are trying to sell them, and how it will be of benefit to them. If you have more than one offer, briefly explain each one. Never, ever just stuff a bunch of flyers in an envelope and send it out. You will only waste your money. I am NOT referring to so-called "Big Mails", which contain numerous unrelated offers. These are different because of the way they are presented. I am talking about you, as a mail order operator, trying to sell something to a prospective customer. Remember, you have just a few seconds to get the readers attention (providing he or she even OPENS the envelope, but that is another topic all together) and you have to not only grab their attention, but hold it long enough for them to read your entire offer. If you have a bunch of sales flyers thrown in an envelope, haphazardly folded, you will not grab the attention of anything except the trash can! So many times I get mail like that and feel sorry for the people making the offers because I know they just wasted their money. Or how about the MLM programs that are abundant today, with the free calling cards? Just a card sent in the mail, with a brief brochure. No cover letter, no return address, no introduction, and no explanation of what they are trying to sell you! This is a waste of money to the mailer! Take some time to explain why you are offering somebody something, and why he or she needs it!

If you do send more than one offer, be sure to fold them together, not individually. It is a pain in the neck to unfold each flyer individually, and your response rate will suffer. Fold them the same way, neatly, with the headline of the flyer or brochure facing the reader. People usually open the envelope from the top, with the back facing them. You want them to see your headline or first line of your cover letter as they open the envelope.

Once you have a customer order something from you, by all means include a few offers when you send them an invoice. In this situation it is beneficial to include more than one offer because the customer already knows who you are, and obviously trusted you enough to place an order for something. They will take the time to look over your other offers now.

In my experience, I have always achieved better results by including one offer on a blind mailing. I include a killer cover letter, an informative and motivating brochure, and a reply envelope to make it easier for the customer to order. Once I get an order I send an invoice with two or three (never more than that) back end offers. I also send them a catalog. Whatever you decide to do, always test your campaigns. If you are going to send out more than one offer, make sure they are related and always include a cover letter. Mail your offer to yourself and see what it looks like when YOU open it. If you are not impressed, your customer will definitely not be either. Remember, people have short attention spans, and they get confused if there are too many offers that they do not understand or care to understand! I suggest you concentrate on your best offer and mail only that one offer. Use the others as back end sales.

MAKE YOUR OFFERS IRRESISTIBLE

Have you ever ordered something by mail that you really were not that excited about, but the bonus offered to buy was so good that you just could not pass it up? Millions of people order products and services every day simply because of the bonus offered. Great bonuses increase the perceived value of an offer, and result in a greater number of sales!

Think about your own offers. What can you offer as a bonus to your product or service that will entice people to act upon your offer? What will increase its value in the minds of the customer? One of the greatest things to offer as a bonus is something that costs very little yet has a high-perceived value. Information is a great bonus to almost any product. When described properly, information has great value. People will order your product just to receive the bonus!

A great example of this is the bonuses used by major magazines to solicit new subscribers. They offer free videos, books, clock radios, or other products that seem to have high value. They tell you that you can "keep the bonus" even if you are not happy with the subscription. This is great marketing! Does it work? You bet it does. Magazine publishers sell millions of subscriptions just because people want the bonus, not because they necessarily want the magazine. See, if people wanted a subscription, they would have ordered one long ago. But, the bonus made the offer so valuable and interesting that they were moved to action and ordered! This is the key. The bonus offer should be so good, that it makes it hard to say no.

Sure the bonus costs a little bit, but not nearly as much as its "perceived" value. And, since the hardest thing to do is to secure NEW customers, it is well worth the extra expense. Once you have the customer, you can sell them again and again!

Think about your own offers. Can you offer something, information, a product, cassette, or something else? The bonus should compliment your product or service, and increase its value. If possible, guarantee that the customer can keep the bonus, even if they return your product. This gives the customer confidence in ordering. Really think about your offers. You want to take the risk of making the buy decision away from your customer, and make the offer so good that it is hard to say no.

This method of selling works! It works because people feel they are getting something for nothing. They feel comfortable because they are not at risk. They want to know that they can get their money back, and even get a bonus, just for giving your product a try. Sure, some people will take advantage of your free offer and return your product. But, the percentage that does this is very small. Like I always say, you should

NEVER sell anything that you would not be comfortable buying for yourself. So, if your product is good, you will not have to worry about too many people returning it just to keep the bonus. So, go that extra step and offer something of value as a bonus!

Another way to make your offers more appealing is by offering special payment terms. If you have a product that costs $100, offer it for three payments of $33. Since most people are used to buying items on monthly payments, this will increase your sales. By making the product easier to purchase and pay for, you will have an advantage over your competitors.

If you accept phone orders, you may want to get an 800 number. An 800 number can be set up these days for very little money, and will result in increased sales. It is especially helpful if you have a merchant credit card account, and can accept major credit cards. The 800 number, combined with the convenience of credit card payments, will substantially increase your sales!

If you are selling by direct mail, you can increase your sales by including an order form and pre-addressed reply envelope. This eliminates some work for the customer. The more work you eliminate, the more likely they are to order.

Finally, make sure that you put some type of urgency in your offer. You need to give the customer a reason to order-right now! Without urgency in your ad, your customer will be left hanging. Give them a reason to act right away. For example, you might put a time limit on the offer. Or, you might tie it in with your bonus offer and say, "the first 100 people to respond will receive this bonus FREE". Whatever you decide, give them some motivation to act now. Otherwise, the customer will forget about your offer.

Direct marketing is not easy, by any means. People are bombarded with offers everyday for all types of products and services. You want to make yours stand out above the rest. By offering a bonus, making it as easy as possible for the customer to respond, and creating some type of urgency you will maximize the chances that your offer will be a great success! Just always remember, you must offer a good product or service as well. Since customers are so hard to obtain, the last thing you want to do is lose them because your product was no good! The key to success is REPEAT business. So, you must be sure that your customers are satisfied once you obtain them, or you will kill any chance of selling them additional products or services in the future.

SHOULD YOU ASK FOR A SASE IN YOUR ADS?

There's a great deal of debate about whether or not to ask for a Self Addressed Stamped Envelope (SASE) or some form of payment ($1.00, stamps, etc.) in ads. Like anything else in direct marketing there is no clear-cut answer, but certain guidelines that should be followed.

There are two schools of thought on this issue. Some believe that asking for a SASE or payment for further information cuts down on the number of responses you'll receive. Others contend that by asking for some form of payment or SASE you'll receive better-qualified responses from people that really *WANT* the information, because *they paid something for it.* Both have valid arguments for and against, and the answer lies somewhere in the proverbial middle. Let's examine the issue a bit further and you'll get a clearer idea of which practice you should adopt for your own advertising.

First of all, I used to believe that it was always wrong to ask for a SASE or token payment to send people information. However, I quickly learned that it is the ad itself, and not whether or not you are asking for a SASE, which determines response rates. It also depends on just what it is you're advertising! I read an article by a so-called "expert" who said that you should never ask for a SASE or payment in an ad. He claimed that your favorite stores don't charge for admission, and that when you request information from General Motors or IBM they don't ask for a SASE. Well this is a ridiculous statement. True, but stupid. First of all if you *"request"* information from a company like GM or IBM they already know you're interested in their product. Secondly, we're talking about major dollar purchases for a car or computer. It's easy to build in advertising and promotional costs when you're an established company selling high-ticket items. Most direct marketers are selling items of much less value, and don't have huge ad budgets to work with.

The truth is, *if the ad is well written and clearly describes the product or service it doesn't matter if you ask for a SASE or not!* That's right, the clearer your ad is the better your response rate will be, irregardless of whether or not you give the information away or charge $1.00 for it. If your ad is vague, or a "blind ad" (*never really telling the reader what it is you're advertising*) you won't know if the person that responds with a SASE is any more interested than the one who doesn't. The point is that you want *qualified prospects.* These are people that are most interested in what you're advertising. Many people will respond to any ad offering free information, but they are not *qualified inquirers* because they may not be interested in what you're selling. On the other hand, just because they respond with a SASE or small payment doesn't necessarily mean that they're any more interested. They just might like to waste money! *The trick is to make your ad as clear as possible so that you know the people responding are really interested in what you're selling.* It also depends on where you're advertising. Most opportunity type magazines or "inner circle" tabloids and publications have readers that are just looking for opportunities, or operate small, part time businesses. They're accustomed to seeing ads asking for a SASE or small payment and have no problem sending them for information they want to receive.

I believe that asking for a SASE is a good way to qualify prospects for *informational type* products, such as newsletters, reports, books, MLM programs, etc. I've run ads for years for books and my newsletter and can honestly say that there is very little difference in response rates when I ask for a SASE. However, the people that respond with a SASE, stamps, or payments convert to sales almost twice as often as those responding to my ads that ask for nothing do. I attribute this to the fact that they're truly interested in what the ad is selling and are willing to send something to receive further information. Let me emphasize that if you *DO* ask for a SASE or small payment you should send them something worthwhile, not just a flyer. Send professional sales material, a report, or something else that makes the respondent trust you and not feel as though they've been ripped off.

When I sell tangible consumer products I never ask for a SASE or payment for more information. For example, I sell custom made automotive floor mats, and advertise in several different publications. The ad clearly states what we're selling and that we'll send a free brochure to those responding. They can call or write for more information. In this case we know that the potential customer is interested because the ad is clear. Plus, the mats cost a minimum of $60, so they are a rather high-ticket item. There's no need to ask for a SASE or small payment because in this case it *would* affect our response rate. People don't want to pay for information on *consumer products*. However, if you're selling a moneymaking opportunity people are much more likely to part with $1.00 or so because they believe you're going to show them how to make a lot of money.

So, after all this discussion what do I suggest? If you're selling tangible products it's not advisable to ask for a SASE or small payment. If your selling an "opportunity" it is an acceptable practice and will in fact result in more qualified prospects. I'll take 10 orders from 20 respondents over 10 from 100 any day. Mail order dealers selling opportunity offers are usually small companies that don't have a lot of advertising money. Test your own ads both ways and see which works best for you. Remember, the key is sales per inquiry, not total responses!

SAVE UP TO 17% ON ADVERTISING COSTS!!

In mail order, it is a known fact that your largest expenditure, and the most important for your success, is advertising. Without effective advertising, it does not matter how good your product or service is, it will not sell. There is an old saying that says if you do not advertise, a terrible thing will happen-NOTHING! That's right, you must advertise, and, do plenty of it! Now, advertising is expensive. But, how would you like to save up to $170.00 for every $1,000 of advertising you purchase? This can add up in a hurry, and will allow you to invest in even more advertising to promote your products and services.

There is a simple, legitimate way to save up to 17% on your advertising costs which many people do not take advantage of. Some do not realize the opportunity exists, and others believe it is too difficult or complex. What is it? *Form your own advertising agency!* This is a common practice, and it is not difficult to set up.

Once you form your own advertising agency, you can take a discount allowed by almost all publications. A 15% discount is allowed if the ad is placed through an advertising agency. An additional 2% is given by many publications if payment is received up front for the ad, or within a given 10-day time period. Look at the ad rate sheet for any given publication to find out what their requirements are for a cash discount.

While not all publications give a 2% cash discount, most will give the 15% advertising agency discount. This is given for classified ads as well as display ads. The savings can really add up, giving you more available funds to place additional ads! Think about it. If you place $1000 worth of advertising, your cost will be only $850 by placing the ad through your own in-house advertising agency. If the publication gives a 2% cash discount, you save an additional $17. So, your total savings will be $167! As you can see, over the course of a few months, your savings will be substantial!

It's not difficult to set up your own in-house advertising agency. In fact, it's simple, and perfectly legal. All you have to do is think of a name different from your company name, and get some letterhead printed for your new ad agency. When you submit your order for advertising, simply send it in on your ad agency letterhead, and claim the 15% discount! Submit the ad using an "Advertising Insertion Order Form". This makes the ad order more professional looking. A sample ad insertion order form will look something like this:

YOUR LETTERHEAD HERE
AD INSERTION ORDER

Date: Order No.:

_____This is an order for a Classified Ad.

_____This is a space order for a Display Ad.

Name Of Publication:_____

Date Or Issue In Which Ad Is To Be Run: _____

Number Of Words Or Space Size:_____ Cost:_____

AD Copy:

Category/Heading For Placement: _____

Gross Cost Of Ad: _____

Less 15% Agency Discount: _____

Net Price For Ad: _____

Less 2% Cash Discount: _____

Total Due: _____

Authorized By:_____

This form is one example of an ad insertion and can be adapted to meet your particular requirements.

Your new agency will not have to be registered, since it is not generating income or expenditures. You can open a checking account under your ad agency's name, or simply pay for the ads via money order so that the publication recognizes the agency separately from your company. Do not worry that the publication knows it is an in-house agency. It is a common practice, and almost all publications will honor the discount. So, take the simple step and form your own in-house agency right away! It will save you a lot of money! *You can even place ads for others and make a profit!*

SIX WAYS TO GET FREE PUBLICITY-WITHOUT PRESS RELEASES!

It's common knowledge that the use of press releases is the number one way for you to get free publicity for your products and services. I've written about how to create and use press releases on numerous occasions in the past. If you're not using press releases, you are simply not serious about generating publicity for whatever it is that you're selling, it's as simple as that.

However, press releases are just ONE way in which you can generate free publicity. Yet, they are certainly not the ONLY way, nor are they always the most effective. Savvy marketers use many other techniques to generate free publicity. I want to share with you six other strategies for generating free publicity that you may or may not have thought of. I've used, and continue to use, these in my own marketing efforts with a great deal of success.

THE INTERNET

Yes, that wonder of communications technology that's turning an entire country into a bunch of computer geeks. But seriously, whether you like the Internet and its influence on society or not, the truth is that it's a MAJOR source of free publicity. There are several places where you can set up a free web page (**www.freeyellow.com** is one of the best). There are also several places where you can place free ads, product releases and information about your company. However, these are rarely successful because there are so many references on the Internet that the chance of your free ad or web page being found are slim.

A better strategy is to join some on-line discussion groups dealing with your subject matter. For example, if you're selling a book on home gardening you might want to join a discussion group dealing with gardening. Once you're in there, it's easy for you to plug what it is you're selling. You can also post ads and/or promotional information regarding your products and services on one of the numerous free Billboards that are on the Internet. These, like discussion groups, are an excellent way to get your information into a targeted group of prospects.

DIRECTORY LISTINGS

There are hundreds of directories available covering any number of products and services. Visit the reference section of your library and you'll be amazed at what you'll find. The Thomas Registers (listing of manufacturers and marketers of industrial and consumer products) Drop Shipping Directories, Wholesale Products Directories, Gift Directories, Business Handbooks, the list is endless. Many of these directories make their money by selling the directory and offer free listings to companies that supply products or services geared toward their markets.

For example, if you were selling that home gardening book you might get a free listing in a directory of gardening suppliers. The point is, whatever you're selling, chances are that there is a directory reaching your target market. Get yourself listed in as many as you can.

You can also contact other marketers of products and/or services similar to yours. Ask them if they would consider throwing in your brochure or sales materials with the orders they fill in exchange for a commission or piece of the profits. This is a win, win situation.

FREE REVIEWS

Not having any luck with press releases? Try a different approach. Instead of sending a release to the editor, send a sample of your product or service for review. Editors are ALWAYS looking for new products to review and will be happy to give you a free plug–assuming your product or service is worthwhile of course. Newspapers, magazines and newsletters are all excellent places to submit your product or service for review. Just be sure that the circulation base is comprised of people that will be interested in what you're selling.

There are also many syndicated "experts" that review products and services. Check newspapers and magazines for these syndicated columnists and submit a sample of your product for review.

WRITE ARTICLES

Writing articles is one of the best ways to get free publicity that I know of. Once you have a certain level of expertise, and assuming you can write effectively, you can submit articles to publications catering to your target market. Using the aforementioned home gardening book example, you might write an article giving some tips and pointers for growing roses. You can even take a chapter or part of a chapter right from the book itself and make it into an article. Editors are always looking for new material to give to their readers.

Most publications will not pay you for your article, but that's not your goal at this point. You want to get that article printed! The publications will allow you to put a plug at the end of the article (called a resource box) where you can give some information on yourself or company and some contact information. People will read the article, which gives you instant credibility, and if they are interested they'll contact you for more information. My articles reach nearly a million readers each month–how much do you think that is worth in free publicity?

LETTERS TO THE EDITOR

So you're not quite ready to write an article? How about a letter to the editor. Believe it or not, those get read. You might use the trick of referring to an article you read in a previous issue and subtly plug your own product or service. You have to be a bit creative here though. Editors will not run your letter if it appears to be nothing more than an attempt at free publicity. Once again using our home gardening example, let's say you read an article on protecting roses in the winter in Home Gardening or another publication. You could write a letter to the editor and either agree or disagree with something in the article. You might mention that you have a great tip, and mention it's from your new book, which can be purchased from...Bingo!–you just slipped in a free plug for your book!

RADIO AND/OR TV TALK SHOWS

Have you ever sat and listened to a radio or TV talk show and found someone calling in offering a product or service dealing with the subject being discussed? I have. A great example was during the big earthquake out here a few years ago. I was listening to a local radio show and people were calling in giving tips on how to be prepared for the "next one". One guy called in and started talking about his company which would "earthquake proof" your home by anchoring furniture to the walls and sell you a survival kit. He cleverly gave his name and phone number on the air. I bet he got a ton of leads from that short call in.

If your product or service lends itself to this type of promotion by all means use it. It doesn't have to be a national talk show. Check your radio listings for local shows. You can call in and plug your product or service for free. It's like getting a two-minute radio ad spot for nothing!

Getting publicity is a never-ending task. I've discussed six ways that you can get free publicity without press releases. There are many, many more. Experienced marketers are constantly on the lookout for ways to plug products and services. Spend some time working on free publicity. With a little imagination and effort you could easily be generating as many leads and prospects from free publicity as you do from paid advertising.

PLACE ADS IN THOUSANDS OF NEWSPAPERS FOR JUST A FEW DOLLARS EACH

There is a little known way to place classified and display advertising in newspapers all across the nation and save up to 50%! For example, you can place a 25 word advertisement, in 184 New York newspapers, with a total circulation of over 1 million readers for under $200.00!! You can realize similar savings from each and every state!

The secret? Use state Press Associations to place your ads for you. These associations place Ads in all of the state's newspapers for you! These are called S.C.A.N. ads (State Classified Advertising Network). Think about it! You place ONE ad to the association, and they place it in hundreds of newspapers for you-at a savings of over 50% off regular rates!

Most Press Associations are easy to work with. However, most will not accept ads for work at home programs. But, if you are selling certain books, or products, it is an excellent way to reach a huge audience.

Contact the Press Association in the states for which you wish to advertise. Following is a listing of Press Associations for each state. This list was current as of the printing of this book.

STATE PRESS ASSOCIATIONS

Alabama Press Association, 3324 Independence Dr., Suite 200, Birmingham, AL 35209, 205-871-7737

Arizona Newspapers Association, 1001 N. Central Ave., Suite 670, Phoenix, AZ 85004-1947 Fax: 602-261-7525

Arkansas Press Association, 1701 Broadway, Little Rock, AR 72206 501-374-1500 Fax: 501-374-7509

California Newspaper Publishers Ass., 1311 I Street Suite 200, Sacramento, CA 95814 916-449-6000

Canadian Newspaper Publishers Ass., 890 Younge St. Suite 110, Toronto, Ontario M4W 3P4 Canada 416-923-3567

Canadian Community NewspaperAss., 90 Eglinton Ave. Suite 206, Toronto, Ontario M4T 2Y3 Canada 416-482-1090

Colorado Press Association, 1336 Glenarm Place, Denver, CO 80204 303-571-5117

Florida Press Association, 336 E. College Avenue Suite 103, Tallahassee, FL 32301, 904-222-5790

Georgia Press Association, 366 Mercer Univ. Dr. Suite 200, Atlanta, GA 30341, 770-454-6776

Illinois Press Association, 1 Virginia Ave. Suite 701, Springfield, IL 62704, 217-523-5096 Fax: 217-523-5134

(Indiana) Hoosier Press Association, 300 Consolidated Building, 115 N. Pennsylvania St. Indianapolis, IN 46204 317-637-3966

Inland Daily Press Association, 777 Bussee Highway, Park Ridge, IL 60068, 847-696-1140

Iowa Newspaper Association, 319 East 5th, Des Moines, IA 50309, 515-244-2145

Kansas Press Association, 5423 S.W. Seventh, Topeka, KS 66606, 913-271-5304

Kentucky Press Association, 101 Consumer Lane, Frankfurt, KY 40601, 502-223-8821

Louisiana Press Association, 404 Europe St., Baton Rouge, LA 70802, 504-344-9309

Michigan Press Association, 827 North Washington Avenue, Lansing, MI 48906, 517-372-2424

Mississippi Press Association, 351 Edgewood Terrace, Jackson, MS 39206, 601-981-3060

Missouri Press Association, 802 Locust, Columbia, MO 65201, 314-449-4167

Montana Press Association, 1900 North Main St. Suite C, Helena, MT 59601, 406-443-2850

National Newspaper Association, 1627 K Street NW Suite 400, Washington, DC 20006, 202-466-7200

Nebraska Press Association, 1120 K Street N.E., Lincoln, NE 68508, 402-476-2851

Nevada State Press Association, P.O. Box 1030, Carson City, NV 89702 702-882-8772

New England Newspaper Association, 70 Washington St., Salem, MA 01970, 617-744-8940

New England Press Association, Suite 280-HN 360 Huntington Ave., Boston, MA 02115, 617-437-5610

New Jersey Press Association, 206 W. State Street, Trenton, NJ 08608 609-695-3366

New Mexico Press Association, 150 Louisiana N.E. Suite A, Albuquerque, NM 87108, 505-275-1377

Newspaper Advertising Bureau, 6180 Avenue Of The Americas, New York, NY 10036, 212-704-4500

Newspaper Association Of America, P.O. Box 17407, Dulles International Airport, Washington, DC 20041, 703-648-1000

New York Press Association, Executive Park Tower, Albany, NY 12203, 518-482-0400

New York State Publishers Association, 11 N. Pearl St. Suite 1207, Albany, NY 12207, 518-449-1667

North Carolina Press Association, 4101 Lake Boone Trail Suite 201, Raleigh, NC 27607, 919-787-5181

North Dakota Newspaper Association, 222 N. 4th Street, Bismark, ND 58501, 701-223-6397

Ohio Newspaper Association, 1225 Dublin Road, Columbus, OH 43215, 614-486-6677

Oklahoma Press Association,3601 N. Lincoln, Oklahoma City, OK 73105, 405-524-4421

Ontario Community Newspaper Assoc., 1184 Speers Rd., Oakville, Ontario L6J 5A8 Canada 416-844-0184

Oregon Newspaper Publishers Assoc., 7150 SW Hampton St. Suite 232, Portland, OR 97223, 503-684-1942

Pennsylvania Newspaper Association, 2717 North Front, Harrisburg, PA 17110, 717-234-4067

South Carolina Press Association, Box 11429, Columbia, SC 29211, 803-254-0345

South Dakota Press Association, P.O. Box 2230, Brookings, SD 57007, 605-692-4300

Southern Newspaper Association, Box 28875, Atlanta, GA 30328

Suburban Newspapers Of America, 111 East Wacker Dr., Chicago, IL 60601, 312-644-6610

Tennessee Press Association, Box 8123, Knoxville, TN 37996, 615-974-5481

Texas Daily Newspaper Association, 8 San Jacinto Blvd., Suite 1250, Austin, TX 78701, 512-476-4351

Texas Press Association, 718 West Fifth Street, Austin, TX 78701, 512-477-6755

Utah Press Association, 467 East 3rd South, Salt Lake City, UT 84111, 801-328-8678

Virginia Press Association, P.O. Box C-32015, Richmond, VA 23261-2015, 804-648-8948

Washington Newspaper Publishers Ass., 3838 Stone Way North, Seattle, WA 98103, 206-634-3838

West Virginia Press Association, Suite 200 101 Dee Drive, Charleston, WV 25311, 304-342-1011

Wisconsin Newspaper Association, Box 5580, Madison, WI 53705, 608-238-7171

Wyoming Press Association, 710 Garfield, Suite 248, Laramie, WY 82070, 307-745-8144

USING DIRECT MAILINGS WITH ADVERTISING

You've got to fire away with both barrels. No, I'm not referring to hunting. Like I always tell my friends that hunt, I'll consider hunting a sport when the animals are able to shoot back. I'm talking about your marketing efforts.

One of the most frequent questions I'm asked is *"should I start with direct mail or by placing ads"*? The truth is, you need to do a bit of both—"fire with both barrels" if you will. Unless you have thousands and thousands of dollars to spend right away, you need to balance your direct mail efforts with an effective advertising campaign. Don't listen to those promoters of mail order programs that tell you to immediately start mailing out thousands of letters. This is a mistake many people make and they end up losing a lot of money. Don't let it happen to you. Yes, it's true that the direct mail route can put some money in your pocket quickly, but ONLY if your mailing effort is effective. More importantly, what you're selling must have enough of a profit margin to make you money! This is where many direct marketing programs fail. You can lose a lot of money in a hurry if you don't do a careful cost analysis to see how many orders you'll need to make a profit. So, where do you start? I've had the most success by starting out with small ads—no matter what it is that I'm selling. A cleverly worded classified ad can draw a lot of responses at a relatively low cost. However, you must be careful to avoid…

THE BIGGEST MISTAKE IN ADVERTISING

What is it? *Trying to sell something directly from a classified or small display ad.* Don't do it, you'll only waste your money. There is simply not enough space to effectively try and sell a product or service. The whole point of a classified or small display ad is to GET PROSPECTS! That's all you want to do. Word your ads in such a way that the people responding are going to be interested in what you're selling.

Start Small–Build Big!

Before you start mailing tons of sales letters, I suggest that you start out by placing some small ads to get interested prospects for your product or service. When they respond, then you hit them with a dynamite sales package to close the deal. This is the classic "two step" method of marketing and it allows you to maximize your marketing budget while testing your sales materials. And don't think that sending the prospect your sales package just one time is enough. You need to follow up with at least two more letters trying to close the sales. If the prospect doesn't order after the third try, file them away and try to sell them something else at a later date.

Believe it or not, many times a classified ad will outpull a small display ad. The reason? Display ads are dispersed throughout a publication's editorial pages. Unless the ad is 1/6 of a page or larger, they tend to get "lost" as the reader flips through the pages. A classified, on the other hand, is in the back with all the other classified ads. People go to the classifieds to **read** them! In major magazines even a 1" display ad can be very costly. Classifieds cost much less and can bring in just as many, if not more, responses. So before you splurge on a display ad that can eat up your ad budget, start with small classifieds. As your business grows, you can increase your ad budget and start placing display ads. Start small, and don't listen to advertising sales people that try to force you into larger size ads or more issues than you want. The classic *"you must try an ad in at least three issues to see if it works"* line is a bunch of hooey in my opinion. If an ad is going to work, it will work the first time, believe me. If the ad's a dog, and you've committed to three issues, you've wasted a lot of money.

Now–Fire The Other Barrel! Once you've started placing ads, add some direct mail to your arsenal. Start with some smaller mailings. You can test a direct mail package to as little as 500 prospects, although 1,000 is better. Mailing out to a list of 100 or so is OK if that's all you can afford, but it's not going to give you much of a barometer to gauge your marketing efforts against. Make sure you are mailing to a list that is geared toward what you're trying to sell. Amazingly, the list you buy can sometimes be *too good!* That's right. If you're trying to promote some pyramid, gifting program or chain letter scheme to a list of buyers of more expensive, legitimate business opportunities, your mailing will bomb terribly. You'll blame the list, when in fact it was what you were trying to sell that was flawed, not the list. Take the time to make sure that the people to whom you are mailing have expressed an interest in, or have purchased, what you are trying to sell.

Now—Fire Both Barrels At The Same Time! Now it's time to use advertising and direct mail together. An effective ad campaign can bolster your direct marketing efforts and vise versa. Why? Because of the recognition. When you place ads, even if they don't make a dime, they can help you get your name and message out to your potential buyers. Now, if they happen to receive one of your direct mailings, suddenly you have some perceived legitimacy because of your advertising. Major companies spend a fortune in advertising geared toward brand recognition. They are not trying to sell you anything; they just want you to recognize the name when you go shopping. Mail order is no different. The more your name is in front of your target market the better chance you have of building some name recognition, which helps translate into sales.

So, remember to "fire both barrels" as you pursue your marketing efforts. Use a combination of both direct mail and two-step advertising in your next marketing campaign. You will have a much better chance of success.

As you become more and more involved in direct mail, you can save postage by applying for a bulk mail permit. A permit costs about $100 a year, but your postage can be as low as 18¢ or so per piece. You only need to do a minimum of 200 pieces for a bulk mailing. You can also get a Pre-Sorted First Class mailing permit, which gives you the benefit of first class at a lower rate. Contact your local post office for information on Bulk and First Class mailing permits.

USING POSTCARDS FOR DIRECT MAIL

If you don't want the expense of sending out a complete direct mail package, you can use postcards. Postcards are cheap to produce and cost just 21¢ each to mail as of this printing. Information type or other mail order products are excellent to promote via post cards because you can actually place enough information on the postcard to really hammer home your product's benefits. They are also great to use for generating sales or inquiries for your "front-end" products. If your product is less than $10 or so you could even try to sell it directly from the postcard.

Postcards are most effective for getting prospects though. For example, let's say you are selling a book on natural ways to lose weight fast. You can send out a postcard, with a powerful "blind" sales message, such as **"Learn How To Lose Weight In Five Easy Steps–Without Drugs, Potions Or Pills!"** Ask for $2.00 and, when people mail in your postcard, send them a small booklet explaining how to lose weight, but really selling them on your bigger, more expensive book. You'll make a little on the front end because you can easily fill this "package" for under $1.00. However, the real money will be made on the "back-end" as people order your book.

INTERNET ADVERTISING HOW TO MAKE IT WORK

Advertising on the Internet is not all it is cracked up to be. Yes, there are 50 million people on the Internet, and growing everyday. And yes, people access the Internet to find goods and services, information, and almost anything else you can think of.

However, when you place an ad on the Internet, or create your own Web page, it does not just magically "appear" before all those people that access the Internet. No, the truth is they have to find YOU. Think of the Internet as a giant highway system, with several different interconnecting major highways, with exits and smaller highways and roads branching off of it. Think of each "exit" as a Website. From these exits, there are smaller links, which lead to other Websites. And, within each Website are several smaller "roads" which lead to several different locations. But, like any highway system, people are not going to find you unless they know that you exist.

If you think that you are going to create your own Web page, or place an ad within somebody else's and have customers flooding you with inquiries and orders you are mistaken. It takes a lot of work to PROMOTE your location on the Web! You see, when people are looking for things on the Internet, they use what are called "search engines". These search the Web for key words or subjects and then list all the Websites that contain the information you are looking for. So, if you are promoting anything, it is imperative that you get listed by one of the search engine companies. If you are placing an ad, make sure that the site that contains your ad is listed with a search engine, and that your subject matter is listed. This is not always easy to do. Even when you are listed, the chance of people finding you is small, especially if you are listed under a popular information category. For example, I did a quick study the other day on moneymaking opportunity categories. Check out the number of Websites or locations for information on each of the following five categories:

Category	Number Of Listings
Mail Order	500,762
Home Business	712,918
MLM	141,504
Business Opportunities	224,203
Money Making Opp.	111,011

As you can see, your ad or Website can be lost very easily. Most search engines list 10-25 Websites with each search page. So, if you are on the top of the search list, you might get noticed. But, what if you are 100,000 or more names down? It would take FOREVER for someone to find you. How can you take advantage of the opportunities on the Internet and achieve some response? The answer is that you need to use the Internet as a compliment to your regular advertising programs. If you have a Website, promote it in all your ads and literature. Give people your "address" on the Web so that people can find you. If you are placing classifieds or display ads on somebody else's Website, make sure that THEY are promoting the site. You should promote it as well! Otherwise, nobody will know you are out there unless they accidentally find you. The other thing you must do is get other people to create "links" from their Websites to yours, and you return the favor. These are kind of like electronic referrals. This way, if someone visits a Website that offers similar goods or services as you, they can just click on a "link" and they will be automatically connected to your site! The Internet IS powerful. But do not believe all the hype. Like that great restaurant or truck stop off the beaten path of the highway, people will only visit it if they are DRAWN to it by promotion!

TIPS FOR RUNNING YOUR MAIL ORDER BUSINESS

CASH FLOW-THE LIFEBLOOD OF YOUR BUSINESS

Without a positive cash flow your business will soon die. You must have more cash coming in than going out. Sounds simple, doesn't it? Yet it's amazing how many companies, big and small, new and old, forget about this basic fundamental. A negative cash flow is the number one reason that businesses fail.

Many think making a profit is the most important factor for success. It's a necessity of course, but it's NOT as important as a positive cash flow! Too many people confuse profit with cash flow. Believe it or not, if you have a positive cash flow you can survive even though you are operating at a loss, providing the cash flow continues to be positive! A positive cash flow enables you to survive tough times and perpetuate your business. A negative cash flow will kill your business faster than anything.

Don't confuse profits with cash flow. They are not the same. For example, if you purchase a piece of equipment for $2,000 in November, and pay cash, the *cash outlay* is $2,000. However, if the machine is depreciated over 5 years you might only expense $33.00 in November. I'm not going to go into the details of depreciation and amortization here, that is not my point. I'm just showing you how the "expense" for the month is NOT the same as the "cash outlay". On the other hand, let's say you purchase something for $1,000 on 60-day credit terms. You turn around and resell that item to your customer for

$1,500 on 30-day terms. See the effect on your cash flow? In 30 days you'll be paid $1,500 from your customer. You do not have to pay for the item for another 30 days. For 30 days you not only have your $500 profit, you also have the $1,000 cost to work with. You can invest that money for 30 days in something else to create additional revenue. Even if you made NO PROFIT on the sale, you could still survive because you're working on a positive cash flow. Now you have an idea of what cash flow is, and how it can work, but how do you get it? There are several ways, some obvious, others more creative.

INITIAL START-UP CASH RESOURCES

First of all, if you're just starting out you need enough cash in reserve to use until you start producing a positive cash flow. Very few ventures produce an immediate cash flow! You need to formulate a business plan. Without going into great detail on how to create a business plan (there are numerous books available on this subject) you must figure out your expenses and projected sales. When estimating expenses take into account both fixed and variable expenses. Fixed expenses are those that will not change no matter how many sales you have. Examples of fixed expenses are rent, loan payments, lease payments, salaries, etc. Variable expenses change with sales and/or production. Examples of variable costs are costs of goods sold, commissions, utilities, etc.

Now, add up all your expenses and compare them to projected revenues. Subtract the expenses from your revenues to obtain a projected profit. At the point your revenues equal your expenses, you have your break-even point. If this is one year away, you need enough cash to get you to that point. One note here from personal experience. When you figure your expenses for the first time in any start up venture double your initial figure. That's right, double it! Why? Because you'll underestimate the start-up costs. You'll be amazed at all the new costs and expenses that arise in the developmental phase of any business.

CUSTOMERS, CUSTOMERS, CUSTOMERS!

Face it, the most important form of cash flow is sales! In order to get sales you have to sell more products! Simple concept. Easy to do? No. That is the challenge of any business, to increase it's sales! Spend all the money you can afford on sales, marketing and advertising. If you don't get new customers than the issue of a positive cash flow is mute because you'll soon be out of business. Get customers! Once you get them sell them over and over again! Always offer them something new, and do everything you can to keep them satisfied!

USE YOUR VENDOR'S MONEY

You can use your vendor's money to increase your cash flow. While it may be admirable to want to pay for everything when you buy it, this is not good business. You must negotiate terms with your suppliers whenever possible. Of course, if you're just starting, you might have to pay for purchases up front or on a COD basis until you can establish credit. As soon as you can establish credit, do so. The longer the terms the better. Standard terms are 30 days. However, you can try and negotiate 60 day terms or longer. Once you establish terms you are working on your vendor's money! How? Let's say that you get some sales flyers printed for $500. If you have to pay that $500 up front you are out the money without any revenue-a negative cash flow. However, let's say you get 30-day terms. You now have 30 days to send the flyers out, receive orders, and put the money in the bank. Bring in over $500 in sales and you have a positive cash flow!

USE YOUR CUSTOMER'S MONEY

I do this all the time in my import business. I may sell a customer an order for $50,000 and receive payment upon shipment from the orient. However, I negotiate 30-day terms with the supplier, and also have terms with my freight carriers. So, I get the $50,000 up front but do not have to pay for the merchandise or freight for at least another

30 days. I take that $50,000 and invest it in a short term CD or something else and earn a little interest, while at the same time realizing a positive cash flow.

Lease Equipment, Or Buy On Terms

When you first start in business it's hard to get credit. However, it's not difficult to lease equipment. Lease your computer, copy machine, fax, etc. There are many competitive lease programs whereby you can get equipment for a small, or even zero down payment. Many are "lease-to-buy" options where you get the benefits of a lease and still have the equipment to show for it when the lease is up. How does this improve cash flow? By allowing you to pay each month for the expense instead of paying one big sum and amortizing or depreciating the asset. If you only have $10,000 to start up a business it is far better, from a cash flow standpoint, to have a monthly payment of $200 or so than to plunk down $5,000 to purchase equipment.

Be Careful Extending Credit To Customers

This is so important! You have to be careful extending credit to customers. That is one great advantage of mail order. You usually do not have to worry about extending credit. However, if you're dealing in business-to-business transactions you'll invariably have to offer credit terms. Just be sure that you build the cost of money for those terms into your price. In other words, if you offer 30-day terms charge 1% or 2% more to cover your cost of money. More importantly be sure to stay on top of your receivables! If you don't collect from your customers in a timely matter they can destroy you! I've seen many businesses fail while showing a healthy profit, because their "profit" was tied up in outstanding accounts receivables. This shows the difference between profit and cash flow. The companies had the profit, but not the cash!

SPREAD OUT YOUR CUSTOMER BASE

There's a rule in business called the 80/20 rule. It means that 80% of your business comes from 20% of your customers. This holds true time and again. However, it's dangerous to rely too heavily on one customer. It can end up destroying you. For example, a few years back my company contracted with a Taiwanese company to run their U.S. subsidiary. We landed the largest retail account in the world and thought it was great! They certainly purchased a lot of product, and became 90% of company sales! The production in Taiwan could barely keep up with the requirements, and we were soon spending all our time servicing this one account! We didn't have time to look for new business. Additionally, we had to extend longer credit terms to this account. Eventually, the company could not sustain supplying the customer because of a negative cash flow! So, it's not always a blessing to have large customers. That's another reason direct marketing is a great way to do business. You end up spreading your customer base out over many customers. While you never want to lose a customer, if you do lose one of many you are not hurt as badly as if you lose one of just a few!

These are a few examples of how to increase your cash flow. There are other ways as well, such as cutting expenses and obtaining loans. The problem with obtaining loans is that they have to be repaid!

Now you see the difference between making a profit and surviving! You must have a positive cash flow; I cannot emphasize this point enough. Without cash flow, you cannot survive. Each month you should do a projected cash flow analysis. Write down all sources of revenue coming in for that month, and all expenses. Remember, deal with cash outlays and inlays only, not receivables or accrued expenses-these are profit and loss items. Make sure you'll have enough cash to survive!

SAVE MONEY AND INCREASE YOUR MARKET SHARE BY FORMING STRONG BUSINESS ALLIANCES

Don't be afraid to get friendly with your competitors. Strong competitor relationships are an invaluable asset to your business, and strong alliance can benefit you in certain situations.

I first became aware of this tactic when I was just a kid. My father was a National Sales manager for Westinghouse. Dad was a company man, through and through, and our house was a testament to that. We used Westinghouse® light bulbs, of course, but also had Westinghouse® appliances, radios, you name it. God forbid if somebody brought a GE® or Sylvania® product into the house. I thought he was nuts at the time, but it was also a time in America where people were loyal to their employers, and employers were loyal to their employees (times have sure changed, huh?)

Later on, as a business major in college, I had an opportunity to spend some time with my father in a business setting. He was in town for a sales convention and asked me to join him. I went to meet him at his hotel room and overheard him having a phone conversation, talking in such a way that I thought he was conversing with a long lost friend. He was talking about obtaining a truckload of light bulbs for a major customer and was working out the details of the transaction. I sat there and listened, marveling at how different Dad was in a business situation than at home. It was really my first chance to see the old man "in action" and I was impressed to say the least.

As he finished the deal and hung up he exclaimed with relief that he had just salvaged a million dollar account. *"Was that your Distribution Center?"* I asked. *"No, that was the sales manager of Sylvania®"*, he replied. *"What!"* I exclaimed, knowing Dad's feeling about using the competition's products. *"You mean to tell me you just bought a truckload of lamps from Sylvania?"* He looked at me kind of funny and matter-of-factly told me *"yes, I do it all the time. We didn't have the merchandise, and the customer needed it for a big sale. I bought the lamps from Sylva-*

nia®, and they'll ship them to my customer". I asked if he was worried that Sylvania® would steal the business. He replied that on the contrary the customer would be even more loyal to him because he went out of his way to make sure they had merchandise. To the customer one lamp was as good as the other.

The point of this little story is that there are times when working with your competitors is to your advantage. I learned an important lesson that day; one of many I would learn from my father about business, and have always made it a point to form alliances with my competitors. You can apply this practice to your situation as well, whether you are in mail order, retail, or any other business. There is the obvious practice of obtaining merchandise from a competitor in emergency situations. Yet, there are many other less obvious situations where your competitors can be your friend. Let's take a look at how you can work with your competition to save money and increase your marketing efforts.

FORM A BUYING GROUP

It's no secret in business, the more you can buy, the better pricing you receive. This is one reason that small businesses cannot compete with the big boys. They simply cannot buy as well. One way to overcome this dilemma is to form a buying group with companies that sell similar products as you, but in different markets. Pool your resources in order to receive better acquisition costs. This buying group can be just two companies, or several. The point is that by pooling your requirements you'll be able to buy more merchandise and receive better pricing.

FORM AN ADVERTISING CO-OP

For any business, especially mail order, advertising is the most important component of your marketing efforts. You have to advertise, and the more the better. Unfortunately many small businesses do not have the resources to advertise like they should. I'm not talking about the small ads you place in tabloids or smaller circulation publications.

These are a good place to advertise, but to be successful you MUST get your ads in front of hundreds of thousands of people. How can you do this if you don't yet have the money to place thousand dollar ads, or more? You guessed it, work with your competitors.

Contact your competitors and form an advertising co-op. Maybe you can't afford to place a thousand dollar ad, but you CAN afford a couple hundred bucks. Find four other companies to work with you and now your "Co-Op" can place a thousand dollar ad for $200 apiece. You then split the responses among the five of you. Of course you need to be sure that you're selling very similar things or else there is no use placing the ad. Advertising co-ops are great for mail order businesses because you can work with companies all over the country without considering geographical limitations.

Form A Printing Co-Op

What if you need to print catalogs, sales circulars, or brochures? Work with your competitors to form a printing co-op. It's a fact, the more you can print, the less your per piece printing costs will be. However, catalogs and brochures are expensive to print. If you can work together with some of your competitors that can use the same printed materials, you can cut your printing costs considerably. In printing, the major charge is the set up time to make plates. Once the plates are set up, the per piece printing costs drop considerably as the quantity increases. What you can do is print the same piece, and just change one "block" where the different company addresses are inserted. This charge is minimal and if you do this you save a lot of money on your printed materials.

Share Information

This is another area where it pays to make friends with your competitors. Swap mailing lists, share fulfillment services, and even share employees in some cases. You can check on customer's paying habits, vendor information, the list is endless. There are many areas where making friends with your competitors can really help you.

Of course you still want to have competitive advantages, and there are some things you will not want to share with competitors (proprietary information, marketing secrets, product innovations, etc.). However, don't take this "competition" thing too seriously. I've never been afraid to contact a competitor if it's beneficial to do so. *The point is that there is strength in numbers!*

5 REASONS WHY MAIL ORDER BUSINESS FAIL–DON'T LET IT HAPPEN TO YOU!

In nearly 15 years of business ownership, I've seen many small businesses, particularly those trying to sell via mail order, come and go. Many had a good chance of survival but failed because of poor planning or misguided management. There are many reasons people give for not making it in their own business. However, I believe that there are five major reasons why Mail Order businesses fail. Learn to recognize these and your chances of success will be greatly increased.

POOR OR NON-EXISTENT BUSINESS PLAN

If you do not know where you want to go, how can you ever expect to get there? Many times I've seen people with good ideas never get them to market due to lack of a clear, easily-followed business plan. You must clearly define your goals and objectives and develop a plan detailing how you are going to reach them. This includes projections for sales, income, expenses and overhead. You cannot just *"fly by the seat of your pants"* and hope everything works out for you. It just does not work that way. Without a detailed business plan you'll end up wasting a lot of time and effort and will never realize the true potential of your endeavor.

POOR CASH FLOW

I've written about this point many times in the past, but cannot emphasize it enough. The most important ingredient for any successful business is maintaining a positive cash flow. Without a positive cash flow, your business **cannot** survive, at least not for very long. You may have one month when you do a huge amount of sales, then have two or three months with less revenue than expenses. If you do not maintain the cash flow from the sales in the first month you will not be able to survive the following months. Cash flow cannot be overstated. It is the single most important factor in sustaining a business. I have seen many businesses that had all the elements of success fail because they ran out of funds. Don't let this happen to you. Make sure that you perform realistic and accurate cash flow projections so that you have enough cash resources to fulfill your business plan. Don't guess here. Realistically forecast your revenues and expenses so you'll know just how much money you'll need to operate. Once you determine this, make sure you have enough coming in to meet your expenses!

THINKING THAT SELLING ONE PRODUCT WILL MAKE YOU RICH

It's no secret; the key to success in any mail order business is to establish a strong base of repeat customers. The mistake many people make is thinking that if they can come up with one *"killer product"* and sell it to enough people, they will become rich. This is short-term thinking and is not how you build a successful business. I do not know of any mail order business that can sustain itself, and make a lot of money, by selling only one product or service to a customer one time. You must build and maintain a catalog or portfolio of related products to sell to your customers over and over again. Do not think in terms of products, think in terms of markets! Identify a market with an unfulfilled need, and find products to fill that need. Of course you will need a strong, saleable product or service to attract a customer to make the initial purchase from you. Once that customer purchases something from you, make sure that you have additional products to offer them. If you are selling a service, make sure that it is a something that they will use over and over again, such as advertising or design services. This is truly a case where "more is better". The more related products or services you have to offer to your customers the better your chance of success.

UNREALISTIC EXPECTATIONS

To succeed in business, you have to be realistic. Too many times, I see people that do not have realistic expectations for their business. If you think that you are going to become rich in one or two months, you are most likely not being very realistic. Sure, there is the rare occasion where a business takes off right away. However, in reality you must be willing to stick to a plan and slowly build your business. You must also have realistic profit expectations. Do not think in too general of terms but rather in specific terms. For example, if you are selling something that is automotive related, you obviously have a huge market. Do not think, "If I only get one percent of the market, I will be rich." Instead, strive to sell 10,000 units of the particular item within the first three months. By setting specific goals you are more likely to have realistic expectations.

One of the earliest lessons I learned in business is that no matter how large the target market, there is a tendency to over-estimate how many of a particular item you can sell. This is especially true in mail order. Take chain letters and pyramid schemes for example. On paper, they claim huge potential earnings. However, in reality we know that these claims are ludicrous. When projecting sales, it is better to under-estimate sales then it is to base your plans on unrealistic expectations.

Response rates are often over-estimated in mail order. Successful direct marketers know that a 2% response to a mass mailing is very good! You need to try and break even on your mailings with only a 1% response. Yet there are many promoters that claim you will get a 5%, 10% or even a 50% response! Don't believe it! Be realistic with your response projections for advertising as well. You want your ads to make a profit for you, of course. However, don't expect to get rich by placing one ad in a few publications. You must place your ad in numerous publications, and look at the large picture when deciding if the ad is successful. For example, if you place a $100 ad in a newspaper and make a net profit of $20 in a month, this does not seem like much, right? Wrong! Imagine if that same ad were placed in 1,000 papers a month! Now you're looking at a sweet profit of $20,000! Now you're talking some serious money!

GIVING UP TOO SOON

Every successful businessperson I know had times when they felt like giving up. So many succeeded at the brink of throwing in the towel. This is a major mistake that many people make, especially those who do not have a clear plan, or have unrealistic expectations.

If you truly believe in what you are doing there is never a reason to give up. If you want your own business, do not expect it to make you rich overnight. Start slowly, part-time if you have to. Do not quit a regular job until you are fairly certain that your business will succeed. Most importantly, do not quit on your business. Once you give up, it is very difficult to start again because you feel defeated and frustrated–thinking you will never have a business of your own. It took me over two years to realize a profit from publishing my newsletter. However, I believed in the concept and kept at it, changing things constantly until I was finally able to make a profit. I had a clear plan and did not expect to make a profit for at least two years. I did not have unrealistic expectations, had a clearly defined business plan and did not give up. This is one of the major mistakes people make when trying to start a mail order business, they simply give up too soon. You never know what tomorrow will bring, but if you give up it cannot bring success.

If you want your mail order venture to succeed, make sure that you have a detailed business plan, realistic expectations, enough cash flow to maintain your business, a group of products or services which allow you to have repeat sales to a strong customer base, and keep at it. Do not give up!

INCREASE YOUR SALES WITH STRONG CUSTOMER RELATIONS

It's far easier to get business from current customers than it is to find new ones. You must have back-end sales—sales you make to a customer *after* the initial sale. Once you have an established customer base it is imperative that you look for ways to sell them additional products or services, over and over again. However, even if you have numerous products or services to sell to your established customers, if you don't cultivate the relationship, you'll lose them. Most small businesses are so busy trying to find new customers and performing day-to-day operations that they forget to devote enough time to what's really important keeping *existing customers!* Following are some proven techniques I've used to maintain positive customer relations.

THE 80/20 RULE

I touched on this previously. It's a proven fact that 80% of sales will come from 20% of your customers. It only makes sense that you should concentrate on the 20% that really matter. Of course, you should treat all your customers well, but really go overboard with that upper 20%! After all, they're responsible for 80% of your sales! These are your regular customers and they obviously like you and what you have to offer. You should be extra sensitive to their needs.

BE ACCESSIBLE

There's a misconception that if you have a direct marketing business, you don't have to worry about contact with your customers. This is true to an extent, but not if you want to build a thriving business. While you may not have to meet with your customers face to face, you do have to be there when they need you. In today's marketplace, with so much competition and shady operators, you need to gain your customer's confidence that you are for real. Maintain regular business hours, even if you work from home.

Make sure you have as many ways as possible for your customers to contact you—the more the better. Use them for your *customer's* advantage! Take the phone for instance. Be sure you have a voice mail system, or at least an answering machine, to handle calls when you're out of the office or on the line. You don't want your customers to receive a busy signal when they call! Answer calls in a professional and timely manner. If you answer with a *"hello"* and there's a kid yelling or dog barking in the background, just how professional do you think you're going to sound? Worse yet, if you must put a customer on hold *(try to avoid this whenever possible)* don't leave them there too long! ASK them if they would mind holding and be sure to check back with them every few minutes. There's nothing more irritating to a customer than sitting on hold for a long time, especially if they have a complaint or if they want to place an ORDER! The easier you make it for a customer to order from you, the better your sales will be.

PRESENT A PROFESSIONAL APPEARANCE

Every piece of correspondence you send to a customer should exude professionalism. Be sure you have letterhead, envelopes, business cards, brochures, sales materials, etc. that make you look like a serious company. A "penny saved" on correspondence or promotional items that fall into your customers' hands is not a "penny earned". It's OK to be thrifty, but realize that if your correspondence and sales materials do not make a good impression, you won't either.

BE A PROBLEM SOLVER, NOT A PROBLEM MAKER

I've strengthened many a customer relationship in times of crisis. If your customer has a problem, deal with it and do everything possible to make them happy. Don't deny there's a problem, and don't be too quick to point out that it's the customer's fault, even if it is. Realize the importance of repeat sales and look at the problem from a "future sales" perspective. If you solve the problem now, even if it means losing a little money, chances are your customer will reward you with additional business.

Customers like to hear the truth if the mistake is yours, *but not if it's theirs*! You can nicely point out the facts, and take steps to rectify the situation. However, don't compound the problem by telling the customer it was his or her own fault! Sometimes you might honor a warranty after it has expired, or give the customer a discount. Always weigh the cost to you now against the potential long-term sales from that customer. It's worth a couple bucks today if you receive hundreds or thousands of dollars worth of orders from the customer over a few years.

Now, this doesn't mean you have to put up with abusive, ignorant, hostile customers. The customer is not "always right". Look at each situation individually and handle it accordingly. For example, one time I was doing a job for a client. I established a price, and did what I thought to be a good job–and it was. The customer wanted more and more done, and made ridiculous change requests for the job. I finally told him that it was obvious I couldn't make him happy and that he should take the work elsewhere because it wasn't worth the hassle to me. There comes a time when you just have to accept you cannot make every customer happy and end the relationship with no hard feelings. Chances are they'll respect your honesty and give you more business in the future. If they don't, you don't need those customers anyway.

ONE HAND WASHES ANOTHER

Don't always look at customers from the point of view of what you can offer them. Many times they might have something to offer you. Often, even if you don't really "need" what they're selling, it may be profitable for you to support them.

For example, a subscription to my newsletter costs $27.95 a year. I advertise in many different publications, but obviously cannot advertise in all of them. One of the major business magazines subscribes to my newsletter, even though they certainly don't NEED the information. Because of this, I place advertising with them each month. So for a measly $27.95 per year, they receive thousands of dollars worth of advertising. I give these people preference over others because they support me! See where I'm going with this? I'm not saying you should support everybody trying to sell you something. That would be ludicrous. Realize that there are times when supporting your customers can pay huge dividends for you in the form of sales and profits! You don't even have to purchase something. When you help your customers, in any number of different ways, the return to you can be worth many times what you spend.

KEEP IN TOUCH!

Customers are like old friends; you have to keep in touch with them to keep the relationship alive. Call your larger customers frequently, even if its just to say *"hi, just wondering if I can do anything for you today."* Keep in touch with your best customers (remember the 80/20 rule!) by sending them notices of special sales or events. Offer them special discounts, terms, or premiums not given to "just anybody".

For business-to-business clients, take this practice a step further. Get to know your customers. Clip articles that pertain to his or her interests and send them with a personal note, saying, "thought you might enjoy this", or something similar. Send birthday cards and Christmas cards, all with a little handwritten note inside. This makes your customer feel special. Keep your name and company fresh in your customer's mind. Remember, "out of sight, out of mind". You don't want them to forget you. When it comes time to place another order you want to be sure they order from YOU, and not somebody else. Keep those 20% of the customers that give you 80% of the business happy!

OFFER A MONEY BACK GUARANTEE

Contrary to what many people will tell you, you are not under any legal obligation to offer a money back guarantee. However, it is something I think you should do. Even if you don't offer a money back guarantee, if the customer doesn't like it it's coming back to you anyway. If they pay by credit card they will just contact their credit card issuer for a charge back. Besides, your whole objective is to have satisfied customers so that they continue to buy from you. So, offer a 30-day guarantee and gladly refund any money for returns. If your product is good you will have few returns. Just chalk them up to a cost of doing business.

The greatest reference you can have is a satisfied customer! Learn to treat your customers right, and you'll be rewarded many times over.

ACCEPTING CREDIT CARDS

As your business grows you might consider opening a merchant account and accepting credit cards. It is not necessary when you are first starting out, but at some point it will be something you should do in order to grow your business. Most people are accustomed to ordering products via mail order using a credit card. I know from personal experience that approximately 40% of our orders are ordered via credit card. I do not know how many of those would order if they did not have the option of using a credit card, but the credit card option is convenient and will increase your sales.

On the other hand, obtaining a merchant account is not always easy and there are charges you must pay. As a small mail order company, you will not be able to obtain a merchant account from your bank. You will need to go through an independent company. You will then need to pay a minimum fee every month, plus rental of the terminal or processing equipment, plus a fee for each transaction (called a "discount rate"). So, unless you are doing a minimum of $1,000 a month in credit card sales, it may not be worth it. On the other hand, when you do reach the point where you can afford a merchant account, by all means get one.

A good source for merchant accounts, which we actually use, is: CardService International. You can contact them at 1-800-456-5989.

THE REAL KEYS TO MAKING MONEY IN MAIL ORDER

Before I wrap up this book, I want to give you the REAL basic keys to making money in mail order. Follow these principals and you too will succeed with your own mail order business!

You may have read or heard from all those other "experts" about how to make money in mail order. Truth be told, many of those so-called authorities are not making a dime. How in the world can anyone tell you how to make money when they barely make enough to buy a cup of coffee? What they have is a hobby, and that's fine if that is all you want your mail order business to become.

I'm betting that you want more–you want to learn how to truly earn a LIVING selling via mail order. I won't insult your intelligence with the old standby advice of finding a product people want which fulfills a need, that is a given. If you don't have a saleable product all the secrets and advice in the world are not going to help you succeed. You also see the old cliché about finding someone who's successful and copying what they are doing. This is good advice, but not always realistic. I love to play basketball, but even in my prime if I hung around Michael Jordan every day and learned everything he knew I would never be MJ. Why? Genetics, among other things. In business it's the same thing. Many have more education, knowledge, money or other resources. So, you've got to find your own way.

Of course you have to have persistence. However, you need intelligent persistence. If you keep doing the same things over and over again without success, it doesn't matter how long you stick with it. If you don't learn from your mistakes and change what you're doing, you are never going to succeed. And, of course, you need back-end sales. If you have nothing to offer customers again and again you are not going to be profitable. It takes too much effort to rely on one-time sales to new customers. You MUST have repeat sales.

So, with the basics out of the way, what are the REAL keys to success when selling information via mail order? There are basically four key elements to building and making money selling information via mail order. They are: Profitability, Controlling Your Own Promotion and Marketing, Understanding the Numbers, and Leverage. That's it. If you truly understand these four keys you will succeed. Let's take a closer look…

Profitability: Sounds so simple, yet it's amazing how many people forget about this key element. If you cannot make money selling your information product, it doesn't matter how great your marketing efforts are. The truth is you CANNOT make money selling one product for someone else and only making $10 or so per sale. If it's your OWN product you are never going to make money unless you have a lot of markup built into your price to cover all your expenses.

The rule of thumb in mail order is to sell a product for four times it's cost, providing the market will allow it. With information products this number will be even higher. You can sell a book or course for $40 or so which may cost you just a few dollars to produce. However, the marketing expenses involved will easily push your cost of sales to several times your base cost. Of course, sales prices depend on the market. But if you don't have enough profit built in you are fooling yourself if you think you will be able to build a business. Whether you produce the product yourself or buy it from another source you need to be sure you can make money at a competitive selling price.

Control Your Promotion And Marketing: The optimum situation is to produce your own product, or at least control the distribution of the product. However, you can succeed selling products as a dealer or distributor providing you: 1) have enough profit and; 2) control your own marketing and promotion. Simply using the marketing materials provided by the source of the product is not going to work. You need to control the marketing and promotional materials.

This can be done by creating your own ads, sales flyers, catalogs and other marketing material. You might even change the titles of the books or other information products you are selling. The real key is not WHAT you sell; it's HOW you sell it. Take the time to learn how to write your own sales materials, or have it done for you.

Understanding The Numbers: You hear all the time about mail order being a "numbers game." Sadly, most people don't take the time to really understand the numbers needed to generate a profit. They don't take the time to test before wasting a lot of money. You need to understand that when all is said and done, you will be fortunate if just one out of a hundred people you present your product to will actually purchase it. Yep, 1% and this is sometimes optimistic. So forget about those 5% response rates you see, they are not realistic to a cold list. Of course the response rates go up considerably when mailing to your own in house customer list, which is why repeat sales are so important.

So, what does this mean? It means that if you cannot break even with a 1% response you are probably not going to make enough money to stay in business for very long, much less earn a living. Successful information mail order sellers reach hundreds of thousands of prospects each year. Of course you don't have to reach that many when you are just starting off, but eventually you are going to need to reach massive numbers in order to get enough customers to succeed. So, how do you reach these numbers without having to do mass mailings yourself? By using the fourth and most important key to success…

Leverage: Above all else, leverage is the most important element to selling information, or any other product for that matter, by mail order. Leverage means that you get a whole lot of people duplicating your efforts so you benefit from their participation. For example, instead of you having to try and sell your book or other product yourself, you offer a distributorship and give others a cut to promote it for you. Now you CAN reach huge numbers without mailing yourself. If you have 1,000 dealers mailing 1,000 sales pieces you would reach one million prospects, through NO effort of your own! Now a 1% response rate WILL make you money–lots of it.

There you have it, the four keys that will guarantee you success. Don't ignore them or you are destined to fail.

CONCLUSION

I know that the information is this book may be a little overwhelming at first and is a lot to digest. What I've given you are the real secrets and strategies myself and others have used to build a thriving, successful mail order operation from our home based offices. Along with the other materials sent with this book you have really received a complete course on mail order.

I wish you the best of luck in all your future business endeavors. Thanks for spending the time with me in the pages of this book and I look forward to reading and/or hearing about YOUR successful mail order business in the not too distant future!

0-595-22055-X

www.ingramcontent.com/pod-product-compliance
Lightning Source LLC
Chambersburg PA
CBHW031053180526
45163CB00002BA/816